It's
MAGIC

Jim Drewett
When Jim Drewett was bundled over on the terraces of Plough Lane by a six-foot ten-inch skinhead in the late 1970s, he received a nasty bang on the head. Ever since that day he's been playing, talking (mainly rubbish) and writing about football . . . as well as continuing to follow the mighty Dons (it must have been some knock!). The thirty-year-old worked in local newspapers and magazines before setting up sports writing agency Deadline Features with fellow desperado Alex Leith. His favourite game of all time was Wimbledon's FA Cup win in 1988, although he admits he was in a toilet on the other side of the world when Lawrie Sanchez scored the winner.

Alex Leith
Alex Leith, thirty-one, was born in Newcastle and brought up just outside Brighton, which means his heart is split in two between United and Albion. He became a sports journalist after the lure of the lira saw him spend four seasons in Italy. He also had a spell at Barcelona. The greatest game he ever played in saw Clissold Park Rangers beat some works team 3–2 away, and it was his header that hit the hand of the defender to give Rangers the penalty that led to their winning goal. The greatest game he has ever witnessed saw Brighton beat Sheffield Wednesday 3–2 to gain promotion to the (old) second division in 1977, which, funnily enough, has found its way into the list.

FourFourTwo

It Was MAGIC

JIM DREWETT
AND ALEX LEITH

PAN BOOKS

First published 1997 by Pan Books
an imprint of Macmillan Publishers Ltd
25 Eccleston Place London SW1W 9NF
and Basingstoke

Associated companies throughout the world

ISBN 0 330 34977 5

9 8 7 6 5 4 3 2 1

A CIP catalogue record for this book is available from the British Library.

Phototypeset by Intype London Ltd
Printed and bound in Great Britain by
Mackays of Chatham plc, Chatham, Kent

Introduction

We've all done it. Trudging back towards the pub after a scrappy 1–0 win against fellow relegation certainties, the victory earned thanks to a deflected second-minute goal and eighty-eight minutes of demented defending. 'That was a great game,' we nod to each other knowingly. But one person's 'great' game is another's match from hell. Despite being in a toilet on the other side of the world when the only goal was scored, the greatest game I ever saw was Wimbledon's glorious FA Cup win in 1988, yet without question there are several hundred thousand Liverpool fans who reckon it's unquestionably the most dire ninety minutes they've ever had to sit through in their entire lives.

Sometimes it's different though. There are matches when the quality of the football, the goals, or the sheer drama (and preferably a combination of all three) leave you feeling exhilarated in an altogether different way. Not because your team has won with a last-minute pile-driver, not because you've avoided relegation on the last day of the season for the third year in succession, but because what you've just witnessed was an example of why football is the greatest game on earth. The purest, most beautiful, most poetic and potentially the most dramatic sport on the planet. And when it happens it reminds you why you started watching Shrewsbury or Rochdale, Orient or Wimbledon in the first place. Because of men like Pelé and Bobby Moore. Because of Puskas and Di Stefano, Cruyff and Neeskens, Hoddle and Ardiles, Jones and, er, Sanchez.

Of course, at its worst football can be mind-numbing. I've got a season ticket for Selhurst Park but I don't go there every other Saturday expecting a re-run of the 1970 World Cup final. At its best, though, it is quite simply the greatest game in the world. Nothing comes near it. Often you see moments that remind you of this fact (yes, even at Selhurst) and sometimes you see matches that ram the pure poetry of football down your throat and right into the pit of your stomach. This book is about matches that do that, the greatest football matches ever played.

Who says they're the greatest games? One hundred carefully chosen current and former players and managers, journalists, commentators and pundits, that's who. Football people. We asked them the impossible question – What is the greatest football match of all time? Actually we asked for their top three, which is like asking someone at the British Library to pick out the best book. But what the hell, we asked it anyway. Tommy Docherty wanted time to think about it, Emlyn Hughes immediately said 'Liverpool 3 St Etienne 1, European Cup quarter-final, 1977' as if he were intercepting an opposition through-ball. Frank Worthington picked three games he'd played in himself, so did Steve McMahon (including that well-remembered classic from 1988, Israel 0 England 0). Archie McPherson reckoned the three greatest games of all time involved either Celtic or Scotland, and Oxford fan Jim Rosenthal controversially plumped for the 1986 Milk Cup final (Oxford 3 QPR 0) as his second choice, narrowly edged off top spot by a certain match in 1966. As the replies flooded in, some definite patterns were developing. The inevitable British bias meant Brighton and Hove Albion looked like making an astonishing three appearances in the top one hundred (which has more to do with Alan Mullery's choices than my co-author's loyalties, honest!) and the 1966 World Cup final is still remembered as if it were yesterday (although according to his faxed reply Derby boss Jim Smith believes the score was 3–1 to England).

But, after months of computer calculations and statistical analyses, the final list was drawn up. So here it is, the one hundred 'greatest games of all time'. No doubt you will immediately scour the following pages and discover, to your horror, that your club's famous cup win or record away victory is not included. You will no doubt be outraged at the inclusion of the 1988 FA Cup final, find out my address and threaten my young children. In my defence I can only say that one hundred 'respected football legends' (and Steve Ogrizovic) are responsible, referee Brian Hill chose the 1988 Cup final and I haven't got any children, so clear off. Once you start reading, though, the memories will start flooding back like goals against at Torquay, and I think you'll find it hard to argue with most of our panel's choices and the order they've ended up in. Some matches you may have been at, some matches you'll have seen from the comfort of your armchair, and some you will never have heard of.

There are one hundred matches recalled in this book, through the eyes of those who were playing or watching, that capture everything that makes football the game it is. From the drama of Charlton beating Huddersfield 7–6 back in 1957 (while down to ten men and after being 1–5 down) and the excitement of the 1993 Champions League match when, 0–3 down to Anderlecht at half-time, Werder Bremen scored five times in the second half, to the beauty of the 1970 World Cup final between Pelé's Brazil and Italy. 'We sat there goggle-eyed,' said Don Howe who watched mesmerized from behind the Azteca goal that day. It's games like these that make sense of our obsession with football and allow us to endure (and enjoy) 0–0 draws on freezing cold February nights. At the point of kick-off every game has the potential to be an absolute barnstormer. 'Great' may be an over-used word in football-speak (Mick 'the boy done great' Channon, you have a lot to answer for) but this is a collection of memories and first-hand accounts of matches that are truly worthy of the word. In the words of Danny Blanchflower: 'The great fallacy is that the game is first and last about winning. It's nothing of the kind. The game is about glory. It's about style, with a flourish, about going out and beating the other lot, not waiting for them to die of boredom.'

Jim Drewett

1

Real Madrid 7 Eintracht Frankfurt 3
European Cup final
Hampden Park, attendance 134,000
18 May 1960

The greatest-ever performance by the greatest-ever club side, there's no other way to describe it. On an afternoon which sent shockwaves through the entire footballing world Real Madrid, inspired by the brilliant Alfredo Di Stefano and Hungarian legend Ferenc Puskas, stunned the biggest-ever crowd to witness a European Cup final with football from another planet.

It was Madrid's fifth European Cup victory in the five years since the competition began, but never before had the famous all-in-white team conquered Europe in such style. The passing and movement, the skill and the vision, the finishing of Di Stefano and Puskas (who scored three and four goals respectively) . . . it was breathtaking stuff.

After the match, shell-shocked by what they had just witnessed, the massive Hampden Park crowd refused to leave until the Madrid team had completed a lap of honour and, half an hour after the final whistle, the ground was still full of incredulous Scots. The fact that Frankfurt had beaten Rangers 6–3 and 6–1 in the two legs of the semi-final contributed to the effect the Real Madrid performance had on the crowd, many of whom had turned up in the belief that they would witness the end of Madrid's European domination. After all, any team that could twice put six past the mighty 'Gers was surely capable of toppling the old masters of Madrid.

Sure enough, in a match that Rodney Marsh described as 'the purest game of football ever played' and made Jimmy Greaves say he'd been 'transported to paradise', it was Frankfurt who took the lead in the eighteenth minute through Richard Kreiss. It didn't last long. Eight minutes later the thirty-four-year-old Di Stefano, who seemed to be gliding around the pitch rather than running like a mere mortal, finished off a five-man move during which the ball never left the ground. The Scottish fans roared their approval. By half-time, with Di Stefano and Puskas (who had fled Hungary following the Soviet suppression in the aftermath of the 1956 revolution) supported superbly by the close passing and dribbling skills of home-grown heroes Luis Del Sol and Paco Gento and the invention of Brazilian winger Canario, the Germans were 1–3 down (thanks to another Di Stefano strike and one from Puskas). Puskas's goal, a rising shot from an angle that makes Marco Van Basten's 1988 European Championship final goal look like a simple tap-in, was greeted with half a second of stunned silence before the crowd erupted.

Worse was to come for Eintracht, although as Real swarmed forward the Germans had their chances too, and the most famous victory in the history of European competition had as much to do with the towering Uruguayan centre-half Santamaria and Argentinian goalkeeper Domingues as the breathtaking skills of Di

Stefano and Puskas . . . well, almost. At the start of the second half, the Madrid players swarmed towards the Frankfurt goal in waves of white-shirted precision, and the shots started to rattle into those big old Hampden goals. For thirty minutes Real played football the like of which the 'live' armchair audience of millions across Europe had never seen before. Watching in Hungary during an end-of-season tour, the England team was stunned. Tuned in thanks to a special aerial that could pick up Swiss TV (the match had been banned in Hungary by the Russian government because of Puskas's presence), Jimmy Greaves says the players agreed that none had seen football to equal it, anywhere, ever. Although his fellow countrymen were not privileged enough to witness them, during this awesome spell the Hungarian defector grabbed three goals in fifteen minutes as Madrid ran riot. Then, on seventy-four minutes, it was Di Stefano's turn to complete his hat-trick with a goal of stunning simplicity, and one that epitomized the team and the performance. Straight from the kick-off after Eintracht had scored, Di Stefano picked up the ball. Interchanging with his colleagues, always moving, always demanding the ball back, he one-two'd his way towards goal and then beat Eintracht keeper Loy with a shot from the edge of the box that flew into the bottom corner.

Eintracht's contribution to this mountain of a match should not be forgotten, and Stein's two second-half goals show the German side were themselves always looking to attack. Indeed the Frankfurt side hit the woodwork twice as well as scoring three. It was this attacking philosophy, however, which gave the Madrid players the space to express themselves as they did.

It was to be the last but one of Madrid's European Cup wins, but the following year the team confirmed its nickname of the club kings of the world by defeating Uruguayan champions Peñarol in the first-ever World Club Championship. And although Cruyff's Ajax are generally credited as the inventors of 'total football', the description fits no team better than the Real Madrid side of the late 1950s and early 1960s, inspired by the 'total footballer' Alfredo Di Stefano. Bobby Charlton once said before a Manchester United v. Real Madrid match in 1957: 'To be honest I was glad I wasn't playing. I saw Di Stefano and these others and I thought these people just aren't human. It's not the sort of game I've been taught.' Even more frightening was the fact their game seemed to be completely natural. 'We never had a black-board, and hardly ever talked about our opponents,' recalled midfielder Francisco Gento, 'and this attitude helped us to turn games our way. In the days of Di Stefano we just came to the stadium, put on our shirts, and played.'

Of the famous final, Jimmy Greaves later wrote: 'On 18 May 1960 we league professionals were made to suddenly realize that we were light years behind the best teams in the world. We watched open-mouthed as Real Madrid took on Eintracht Frankfurt. It was a match in a million . . . they conjured up a match of such balletic beauty that it deserved to be set to music.' And Frank McLintock recalled: 'A few days before the Real Madrid match the Scottish Cup final had been held at Hampden and it was a terrible game. At that time the sides of the ground were very open and everyone was coming up with all these excuses about the pitch and, particularly, the swirling wind. In the papers everyone was saying, "How can we play in the Hampden swirl?", then these truly great footballers come along and make a mockery of that by playing the greatest match of all time.'

I was there . . . Billy Bremner

I was sixteen and I'd just signed for Leeds when I went to Hampden Park, stood on the terraces, and witnessed the most incredible game I'll ever see. It was an exhibition of everything that's good about football, and if you speak to anyone who was there they'll remember it like it was yesterday. It was the sort of match you only ever see once in a lifetime.

For the first fifteen minutes it was all Eintracht, and everyone in the ground knew what a good side the Germans were because they'd given Rangers such a thumping in the semi-finals. They had Kreiss on the wing who was causing Madrid all sorts of problems and the awesome Stein up front. The thing is, although Madrid played so well, I think the Germans always believed they could win it and they never stopped going forward. That's what made it such a great game, Frankfurt were such a good team. Both sides were committed to attack, and that's what gave Real the time and space to turn it on. When Eintracht went 1–0 up they could have shut up shop and sat on their lead, but they didn't.

After twenty minutes Real started running the show.

I'd never seen football played like this before, the crowd was enthralled. If you ask me now to name the entire Real Madrid side, I can. Of course Di Stefano and Puskas were incredible but their entire front line was magnificent. I really can't recall a match that comes close to it in terms of sheer class and quality. We couldn't believe what we were seeing. In Scotland, we'd seen many great sides playing against Celtic and Rangers. But never had we seen two such great sides together on the same pitch. And, for once, the crowd didn't have anyone to hate, and people were able to appreciate the quality on show. If Real Madrid had been playing Rangers the fans would probably have admitted, 'Yeah, that Di Stefano, he's all right.'

But the Scots love their football, they are passionate about it, and the crowd was stunned. At the end of the match the Real players started a half-hearted lap of honour, I don't think they knew how the crowd would react. But as they paraded the Cup the roar got louder and louder, it was incredible, and they must have thought, 'Hey, these people really appreciate what we did today.' Afterwards there was this incredible buzz around the ground, like some great fella had been to visit, like Frank Sinatra had just sung. And for days afterwards it was all anyone talked about in Scotland.

I was there . . . Tommy Docherty

I watched the match in a TV studio in Glasgow, I was one of the so-called studio experts for the BBC's coverage, and I'd never seen football like it and I don't think I ever will again. Everything about it was perfect. There were 134,000 in the crowd, mainly Rangers and Celtic fans, and there was no trouble, no hooliganism, nothing. The match was played in a great spirit by two great teams whose only thought was to go forward and attack, and between them they scored ten goals. Even the refereeing was good. I remember thinking that this is the way the game should be played.

I felt before the match that Real would win because they had so many great players, so many internationals, but I never expected ten goals. The thing is that both teams came to win, and it was constant attack from both sides for ninety minutes. I'd seen some great games up until then, some great cup finals, but nothing like this. Di Stefano and Puskas were outstanding. Di Stefano was the maestro: when he played Real played. The crowd couldn't believe what they were seeing, they talked about it for days afterwards and they're still talking about it today.

You look at the money in the game, Ryan Giggs getting a £6m boot deal, and it's crazy. How much hunger have players got when they're on this kind of money? Players who are miles behind in skill and technique than those who took part in this match. They can't even get 50,000 for an international at Hampden Park nowadays. That night at Hampden there were 134,000 and they'd never seen anything like it.

2

England 4   West Germany 2
(full-time score 2–2)
World Cup final
Wembley Stadium, attendance 96,923
30 July 1966

The English people will never, never, never forget 1966 and all that, when they thought it was all over, and it was then. Neither will the Germans for that matter, who are still complaining about the third goal. Thank God for Russian linesmen.

At eleven a.m. on the stormy, rainy morning of host team England's first-ever World Cup final, manager (then just plain) Alf Ramsey announced his team. The mercurial Jimmy Greaves, who had been injured but was now fit, was not in; Liverpool's more industrious but less skilful Roger Hunt was. Industry was the tactical order of the day, Ramsey's revolutionary 4–3–3 formation swamping the midfield and attacking from the middle rather than down the flanks. The 'wingless wonders' had surprised the rest of the world in a series of friendlies before the World Cup, starting the tournament on the back of a seven-game winning streak, including a 1–0 Wembley victory against West Germany. But they hadn't over-impressed in the run-up to the final, not gaining a head of steam until the semi-final against Portugal, which they won 2–1 with two cracking goals from Bobby Charlton, conceding their first goal of the tournament in the process. England's strength had been not making mistakes, and capitalizing on those of their opponents, a tactic Ramsey drummed into his team throughout the tournament build-up.

It was an untypical mistake from left-back Ray Wilson on thirteen minutes that led to West Germany's opening goal. Wilson jumped too early in attempting a headed clearance from Ziggy Held's cross, and instead presented the (orange) ball straight to Haller, whose snatched shot bobbled between a surprised Gordon Banks and a slow Jack Charlton: England were behind for the first time in the tournament. Poor Ray Wilson – it was the only mistake he made in the whole World Cup. But within six minutes Ramsey's men were level, a credit to the manager for teaching his team to maintain their composure and shape after going down. Overath tripped Moore a fair way outside the area. Moore took the free kick quickly while the Germans were organizing themselves and found Geoff Hurst unmarked: he had stolen behind the defence and headed home past Hans 'Dracula' Tilkowski (he was afraid of crosses). It was a move straight out of West Ham manager Ron Greenwood's training sessions, and it sent the crowd wild.

From then on until the end of the half it was cavalier cut and thrust with both teams coming close. Tilkowski palmed a mild Hurst header to Ball who blasted across a gaping goal. Banks made a double save, first from Overath, then from Emmerich. Then Hunt, set up by Hurst, hit a shot straight at the keeper that the man he replaced in the team, Jimmy Greaves, would have sunk like a pint, and the referee blew for half-time. The second half began in calmer fashion, a heavy shower and words of wisdom from both managers dampening the fire of many of the hitherto over-enthusiastic players. Alan Ball's flame, however, burned brighter than most, and it was an example of the orange-haired twenty-one-year-old's tireless running down the right that led to England's second goal, thirteen minutes from time. Ball's shot was tipped round the post by Tilkowski . . . he took the corner himself, and although Hurst's quick-fire shot was blocked by Hottges, the ball ballooned into the air for what seemed an age before falling to Peters, who scored.

With the Germans piling forward England had a great chance to wrap it up when Hunt got possession in the German half, with only one German defender between him and the goal and Charlton and Hurst unmarked to his right. He found Charlton, but hadn't committed the defender and the chance was squandered. But it didn't seem to matter. Wembley roared like never before as victory loomed, and the Germans seemed down and out of the match. Then, a minute from time, disaster struck. Jack Charlton gave away a disputed free kick outside the box while challenging Held in the air. Emmerich's kick hammered into a red wall, careered off Schnelliger's back – or arm – and fell to Held, whose misdirected shot found its way to Weber at the far post and he poked it through Banks and Wilson. A comedy routine with a tragic ending for England. No sooner had they kicked off than Swiss referee Dienst whistled for time.

England were forlorn. If ever they needed a rallying

cry from their manager it was now. And what Ramsey said in the break before extra-time is the stuff of legend: 'You've beaten them once. Now go out and bloody beat them again. Look at them. They're finished.' It worked. England started extra-time like the team who'd just equalized, nearly going in front when Bobby Charlton, free from Beckenbauer for once, hit a shot that diverted to safety via the post and the keeper's face.

It wasn't the only time the English were to strike wood. Ten minutes into extra-time Nobby Stiles hit a ball that looked to be too long. But it was Alan Ball doing the chasing, and the midfielder caught up and hit a cross in to find Hurst from the by-line. Hurst turned and thumped the ball on to the underside of the bar, after which it landed on (as the Germans thought) or over (as the English reckoned) the goal-line, before Weber headed away. The Swiss referee couldn't decide whether it was a goal, so he went over to consult Russian linesman Bakhramov. Russian wasn't one of Herr Dienst's languages, but the linesman spoke no other. With a nod of his head and a point of his flag towards the centre spot, he validated the goal, his eyes having seen what countless action replays have been unable to verify. 'If it hadn't been a goal,' says Hurst, 'Roger Hunt would have gone for the rebound. As it was he just put his hands up to celebrate.'

The Germans were flabbergasted, and couldn't muster a meaningful attack until the dying seconds. But with people famously 'on the pitch', Moore chested down a cross and, instead of hoofing the ball into the fans, took it down, dribbled out of the area and laid an inch-perfect pass to Hurst, running unhindered towards the German goal. 'I just belted it,' says Hurst on the goal that made him the only player ever to score a hat-trick in a World Cup final. And didn't he just, straight past the rooted-to-the-spot German keeper. The World Cup was England's at last, and the images of Moore holding the Jules Rimet trophy aloft and Nobby Stiles toothlessly grinning beside him are indelibly etched into every English person's memory bank – even if they've only ever seen the pictures.

I was there . . . Bobby Charlton

My job was to mark Franz Beckenbauer and make sure that he didn't go anywhere near our eighteen-yard area. Unbeknownst to me he'd been told exactly the same thing about me, and to be honest we contributed very little to the game in a positive way. We spent all the time actually following each other around. But I was quite prepared to accept that because I thought that with the players remaining we were better than them. And we would have won in ninety minutes if we hadn't given a goal away to a dubious free kick in the last minute.

I had no idea how close we were to the end of the game when the West Germans equalized. We kicked off again, the referee blew the whistle, and I thought, 'No, we've still got ten minutes left.' Because I was so focused, I'd never looked at the touchline where they were prob-ably saying, 'Ten minutes, five minutes, two minutes to go.' It wasn't like that because we weren't hanging on, we were just enjoying still playing the game.

In the period before extra-time we were told by Alf that we had been rushing, and that we mustn't make mistakes. They were as tired as us, and it really was physically exhausting. It had rained and the ground was really heavy, plus it was the end of a long, long stint: we'd been playing since the August before. But we always fancied that we had it within ourselves to actually go through pain barriers, and actually push ourselves, and we did that.

Although the third goal was controversial, it was one of many chances we had, and the linesman gave it. I thought at the time the ball had gone over the line. The matter did cloud the fact that we were the best team. We were the best team that day, and we deserved to win. But that fourth goal, again by Geoff Hurst, a real blaster with seconds to go, capped it all. We were the world champions, which was a fantastic feeling. I knew that life for me would never be the same again. And to this day a day doesn't go past without me being reminded that we won the World Cup back in 1966. And here I am talking about it again, which proves the point!

I was there . . . Trevor Brooking

I watched the match at home with my dad. My mum had gone to the hairdresser and he was supposed to be collecting her after the game. He was just getting ready to go and pick her up when the Germans equalized in the last minute and I said, 'Well you can't go and pick her up now.' So she was left waiting there for another three quarters of an hour, but I seem to remember she was very understanding.

I was an apprentice at West Ham at the time so the fact that Bobby Moore, Geoff Hurst and Martin Peters played such an important part in the match made it even more significant for me. Most West Ham fans still reckon West Ham won the World Cup.

I just remember it being very tense. We just didn't want the anti-climax of losing in the final after getting all that way. There hadn't been much optimism about our chances before the tournament but the country had been gripped by World Cup fever, it had captured everyone's imagination.

You couldn't have bettered the game for drama either. With six goals, all coming when they did, you really couldn't have scripted it better. When West Germany equalized at the end of the match it was terrible, not just for my mum, and you felt we might lose it. But in extra-time there was really only one winner, although the controversy will always rage about the goal that hit the crossbar. I always say the best thing to go by is the reaction of the players and Roger Hunt was in a great position to put the ball into the net and he just turned around to celebrate.

That night I went out with a few mates, who were all West Ham fans, and we had a typical East End night out I suppose. There were a few renditions of 'Bubbles', I think, and the celebrations went on for weeks. At West Ham there was a special feeling of pride. We'd had three great years and the club had provided three players for the World Cup winning team, including the captain and the man who scored a hat-trick. It certainly made me think that I was at the best club I could possibly be at, though unfortunately for West Ham fans I think it made them think that they'd clean up every trophy for years to come, which didn't exactly happen.

3

Italy 3   Brazil 2
World Cup second round
Sarriá Stadium, Barcelona, attendance 44,000
5 June 1982

'**W**hen the match ended I had the producer in my ear telling me I had ten seconds to sum up, then we were going to the news,' recalled John Motson of that sizzling afternoon in the Barcelona sunshine. 'And I remember thinking, "But my goodness, this *is* the news."' Sitting beside Motson in the commentary box for what Motty describes as 'the most amazing match I've ever seen ... pure theatre' was Bobby Charlton, but when the final whistle blew Charlton couldn't come to the microphone. 'He was in tears,' explained Motson.

Unlike the World Cup format today, having got through the initial group stage, the teams had another group to negotiate, the winners of which went straight into the semi-finals. Up until this meeting of football's superpowers, Brazil had swaggered through the tournament. With Socrates, Zico and Junior in full flow, Brazil finally had a team which could stand up to comparison with the great 1970 side. Playing with the same flair and style as their illustrious predecessors, the boys in the famous yellow and green shirts had won every game they played and were firm favourites to lift the trophy. Brazil only needed to draw against Italy to qualify for the semi-finals.

At the start of the match, apart from the 2–1 victory over Argentina in the previous game, Italy had played with about as much ambition as a gravedigger's apprentice, and their number twenty looked an average striker in a negative team. Paolo Rossi (just back from a two-year ban after a bribery and match-fixing scandal) had started the tournament slowly. The day before the teams met, Brazil keeper Valdir Peres had said that his biggest fear was that Rossi might come to life. His biggest fear was about to come true. After this game Rossi was a legend for life and Italy were on their way to winning the World Cup, and winning it in true style.

In the packed Sarriá Stadium, home of Español, where the fans are right at the edge of the pitch and the terraces rise steep and high all round the ground, the atmosphere in the intense afternoon heat was electric. So was the match. Three times Rossi gave Italy the lead. Twice Brazil equalized and, but for an incredible last-minute save from forty-year-old Italian captain and keeper Dino Zoff, they would have done so a third time. It was a match that was on a knife-edge from first kick to last. It didn't ebb and flow, it surged and lurched, first one way and then the other. At times the game was played at walking pace, the exhausted players in their sweat-drenched shirts trying to summon yet another attack, at other times it was fast and incisive. It was always precise, always skilful, and every attack threatened a goal.

After just five minutes Rossi sneaked up on the

Brazilian defence and headed Italy into the lead from Cabrini's inch-perfect cross. After twelve Socrates, the forty-a-day Brazilian skipper, was put through by a superb angled pass from Zico and rifled the ball between Zoff and the post to make it 1–1. Brazil were in control now. The samba drums in the crowd accompanied the swaggering South Americans on the pitch. But despite their possession, with Zico and Falcão controlling the midfield, Brazil seemed to have left their killer touch on the coach. Then, thirteen minutes after Socrates' goal, Rossi scored again. Intercepting a sloppy pass by Cerezo, the new hero of Italy pounced, guiding the ball past Peres to make it 2–1. Again the match had swung back Italy's way.

Nevertheless, Brazil knew they only needed a goal and so far in the tournament these hadn't been exactly hard to come by. They pressed and pressed, but at the same time the Italians always looked dangerous on the break and Rossi miscontrolled in the box with the goal at his mercy. Brazil never panicked and when the superb Falcão (who was so distressed after the match that he considered retiring from football) scored his memorable left-foot curler from the edge of the box – prompting the muppet-haired midfielder into a wild demonstration of jumping on the spot – it seemed Brazil would go through for sure. Relaxed now, jubilant even, with the game at 2–2 with twenty minutes left, Brazil continued to push forward in search of a winner. Asking this Brazilian team to defend a lead would have been like asking Pelé to 'play into the channels'. But it was this commitment to attacking football, a commitment which had lit up the whole tournament, which was Brazil's undoing.

After seventy-five minutes Italy won a corner. The ball was only half-cleared and Tardelli let fly from the edge of the box. It wasn't a sweet strike but who should it fall to on the edge of the six-yard area but Paolo Rossi. And with a deft sidefoot Rossi steered the ball into the back of the net. The Brazilians couldn't believe it, finding themselves behind yet again. They surged forward, Italy defended like only Italians can with Gentile practically ripping the shirt off Zico's back, and indeed they nearly scored again on the break. In the last minute Zoff made his amazing save from Cerezo's header and Italy were on their way. Sensationally, red-hot favourites Brazil were out. This side, however, was one not easily forgotten.

I was there . . . Patrick Barclay

I was lucky because at that point I was the number two football writer on the *Guardian* under David Lacey, so David went off to cover England's rather dull progress and I got to follow Brazil. I covered their first match against the Soviet Union when Eder scored with a wonderful goal, and then that thrilling match against Scotland when the Scots took the lead through Narey's great strike and then got thoroughly slaughtered. Then I stayed with the Brazilians as they moved to Barcelona for their group matches with Argentina, with a young Maradona playing in his first World Cup, and Italy.

All the second-phase games in this group were played

in Español's smaller stadium, the Sarria, which was absolutely packed all the time. For the Italy game the stadium was full as usual, mainly with Brazilian fans, but there was a large contingent of Italians too. I vividly remember about half an hour before the kick-off the Italian players came out to have a look at the pitch, which would have been more like the floor of an oven it was so hot, and the Italian fans went absolutely berserk. There were flags and firecrackers, everything. The Italian players looked up and I swear to this day that their chests doubled in size.

The Brazilian fans themselves had been on parade for hours, and the match got under way in an amazing atmosphere. Brazil had played superbly in the tournament so far and I think they believed they had rediscovered 1970. They had in style, but not in substance, and ultimately it was over-confidence that was their downfall. They had a player like Junior, I mean you don't get left-backs with skill like he had any more, but he was making schoolboy errors at the back. Zico had been outstanding but the Italians had put Gentile on him man for man, and I remember writing afterwards that it was marking verging on indecency. Gentile wasn't a dirty player but he must have been horrible to play against, he was like an octopus.

Still, when Socrates scored Brazil's first goal I think most of us in the stadium thought it was the beginning of a Brazilian procession. It was a beautiful goal created by a piece of skill from Zico, and when the ball went in there was a puff of smoke from the line. But it wasn't to be and Italy and Paolo Rossi killed the dream. I saw the game again a couple of years ago in Italy and it made me realize what a good side the Italians were. At the time I thought they'd sneaked through, but it is possible that they were the best team in the world then. Tardelli was at his peak, he had amazing box-to-box drive like Bryan Robson in many ways. Conti gave them width though he never did anything after this World Cup. They had a young Bergomi who was utterly cool throughout the tournament, they had Gentile, Cabrini at left-back who was a great player and, of course, Dino Zoff, who was one of the best goalkeepers of all time. Zoff's save at the end kept Italy in the tournament, and it wasn't the first time.

I've never felt so sad for footballing reasons as I was after that game: it was like being lovelorn, it was like the end of a fling. I still have this feeling of sadness that Brazil didn't go through. After 1982 the exotic went out of football to a large extent. In 1986 people said that Brazil had become more European, but I think really football just became homogenized. Countries from all over the world adopted the same sort of style, except Africa, which is why everyone took Cameroon to their hearts in 1990. During the World Cup final in Pasadena in 1994 I remember thinking how I would have loved to have swapped the match I was watching for that 1982 game.

4

Brazil 4   Italy 1
World Cup final
Azteca Stadium, Mexico, attendance 107,000
21 June 1970

The unstoppable force meets the immovable object. The most attack-minded team in the world against the most defence-minded. Latin flair meets Latin fear. Samba plays *catenaccio*. South America squares up to Europe. The goodies versus the baddies, with the Jules Rimet trophy for keeps for the winners. This match really did have it all, including, in a period when Italian door-bolt tactics were spreading round the world, the right result. This was Pelé's swansong, and the Black Pearl scored one goal and set up another, but it was the cigarette-smoking midfielder Gerson, finally coming to terms with replacing national hero Didi, who really masterminded Brazil's victory.

The dour Italians had surprised everyone by scoring four goals against West Germany in their marathon semi-final four days before, but any hopes of them coming out and attacking Brazil proved unfounded, especially as they were still tired after their previous exertions in the midday sun. So instead of trying to capitalize on the frailties that undoubtedly existed in the Brazilian defence, they decided to let the South Americans test out the resilience of their own back line. The game was Brazil's for the taking, and they duly came out and took it, though they did have the decency to leave the best to last just to keep the spectacle going.

And what a spectacle. On eighteen minutes the carnival crowd, all yellow, green and blue, lifted the samba rhythm up a gear as Pelé scored, rising high above two Italians to meet Rivelino's cross and plant the ball home. In doing so he became only the second man to score in two World Cup finals. The Brazilians upped the tempo. But while they were startlingly original in their approach play, they were finding it hard to apply the finishing touch, especially when it came to the numerous free kicks the hack-happy Italians were giving them on the edge of the box where a dead-ball opportunity had long been regarded as almost a penalty for the Brazilians. Numerous kicks were blasted over the wall and into the crowd, with Rivelino unusually profligate. The Italians, meanwhile, with Mazzola and Boninsegna linking well, also looked neat, but never threw enough men forward seriously to trouble their opponents. Then, almost inevitably, Cloadaldo, too cocky by half, backheeled the ball to an Italian in his own half. Boninsegna couldn't believe his luck, and his momentum took him past the wrong-footed Brazilian defence and goalkeeper Felix, who'd rushed out too far, allowing him to tap into a naked net. Amazingly, it was level at half-time.

After such solid Brazilian domination, and then self-destruction, this was the time the Italians might have pressed forward to capitalize on a demoralized Brazil. Maybe it was down to tired legs, maybe they just couldn't believe their luck at still being in the game. Whatever the case, they didn't, and slowly but surely the South Americans got back into the samba swing of things. On sixty-six minutes Gerson, ruling the roost in the centre and a role model for smokers the world over, received the ball in midfield, danced to the edge of the box and slammed an unstoppable left-footed shot past Albertosi. Then, just five minutes on, Pelé tapped a Gerson free kick into the path of the onrushing Jairzinho who half ran, half bundled the ball past the hapless Italian keeper. It was his seventh goal of the tournament, and he remains the only man in history to have scored in every game of a World Cup finals tournament.

The Italians were dead and buried, especially as they were unable to react to the Brazilian goals with meaningful attacks of their own. Even manager Valcareggi seemed dispirited, bringing inside-forward Gianni Rivera on for Boninsegna, the only *azzurro* who'd caused the Brazilian defence any problems. Another Brazilian goal seemed inevitable, and when it came, three minutes from time, it was a stunner, becoming probably the most replayed goal in the history of the game. The Brazilians worked the ball cannily out of defence, all one-touch passes, to find Jairzinho, as ever, roaming the wing. He passed to Pelé on the edge of the box, who spotted skipper Carlos Alberto steaming towards the goal down the right. Pelé's arrogant pass was weighted to perfection: Alberto didn't even have to break stride before thumping the ball joyously past the keeper. Talk about aplomb. The first poor Albertosi saw of the ball was when he turned round to see it fizzing into his net.

Minutes later Alberto kissed then raised to the crowd the foot-high solid gold Jules Rimet trophy which now, after three World Cup wins, belonged to his country. But the most enduring images are of Pelé, bare-chested, being carried shoulder-high round the stadium by a huge pack of Brazilians. It was his last appearance in the World Cup, and signalled a wonderful end to a wonderful international career.

A few years later the Jules Rimet trophy, the reward for Brazil's cavalier flair and skill, and since the 1970 final a symbol of it, was stolen from its display case at the Brazilian FA and was never recovered. Even the Brazilian thieves are more skilful than their counterparts around the world, it would seem.

I was there . . . Don Howe

I went out to watch the 1970 World Cup with a group of English managers and it was a real eye-opener. There were people like Bobby Robson, Dave Sexton and Tony Waddington from Stoke. The idea was just to go out there and watch the World Cup, not to look at players to buy, that just didn't happen in those days, it never crossed our minds. We went to look at new tactical ideas, new formations and new training methods.

We were based in this lovely hotel in Guadalajara, and every morning we'd get on a coach, grab a case of beer, and go, 'Right, let's go and watch Brazil', and we'd just go and watch them train. It was so hot and there were so many games that they weren't doing heavy training, just fine-tuning their game. I remember watching

Rivelino firing crosses in from the left wing for Pelé, and he was powering these headers in like bullets. Bang, bang, bang every time. And this went on for ages. We watched Jairzinho practising beating the full-backs and getting in crosses from the right. The coach, Mario Zagalo, stood in as the defender and he'd skin him every time and get in a perfect cross. He did this for about twenty or thirty minutes.

They all seemed to have this incredible application to improve themselves. There was no real coaching as such, Zagalo was just walking around, like it was up to the players what they did. They were all working on their own game, and of course the first goal in the final was a Pelé header from a Rivelino cross from the left, just like we saw in training.

Tickets for the final were hard to get, and there was no way we were going to get director's box type seats. We ended up behind the goal, about ten rows back in amongst the fans. As soon as the game started you could tell that Brazil were on song. You sensed that they were bubbling. The passing and the running off the ball was brilliant. They knew the Italians would play with man markers and a sweeper and so they were moving around all over the place, dragging the Italians everywhere and then players would come up from the back and use the space. They were very well organized, you see. People always say, 'Oh, the Brazilians, marvellous flair players', which is true, but don't kid yourself, they were very well organized at the back too. Anyway, we were mesmerized. We were sitting there goggle-eyed. There was Rivelino, Jairzinho, Pelé. Gerson's diagonal balls to Pelé were incredible, they were like Exocet missiles. And that last goal, I mean what a goal. All those passes and then Pelé just lays it off for Carlos Alberto and he hits it into the bottom corner like an arrow. Pelé's goal was fantastic too, it went in right in front of me. He got so much height from a standing start, it was an incredible jump.

That tournament and that match was an education for me. I was assistant manager to Bertie Mee at the time and for me that trip to the 1970 World Cup finals was part of my coaching education, it was the kind of experience money couldn't buy. I went back to Arsenal and I tried not to get carried away. I mean we'd been doing OK. But I remember talking to John Radford and Ray Kennedy and saying, look, if Tostão can hold the ball up like he does and he's only small, then you big lads must be able to do it.

5

Italy 4   West Germany 3
(full-time score 1–1)
World Cup semi-final
Azteca Stadium, Mexico, attendance 80,000
20 June 1970

The turning point of this match came early into injury
time in the second half. Franz Beckenbauer, surging
towards the Italian goal with the score at 1–1, was
cruelly brought down just outside the box when he
surely would have scored and earned his team a second
successive World Cup final. As it was West Germany
wasted the free kick, Beckenbauer was injured, and the
match went into extra-time, the second time the
Germans had to undergo that marathon in three days
after destroying the English in Leon. With all of the
German substitutes already used Beckenbauer, national
hero as he was (and is), refused to go off, playing the
extra half-hour with his arm strapped up in a sling despite
having (it was later revealed) dislocated his shoulder. But
he couldn't stop Italy from snatching the tie in a thrilling
finale.

It was a classic born of a bore. Italy scored after seven
minutes, which signalled a trench warfare dig-in by the
blue shirts. This was the age when win-at-all-costs
catenaccio was at its height – and the Italians were the
inventors, and the masters, of the tactic. They had quali-

fied from their group in Mexico, for example, by snatching a 1–0 win in their opening game against Sweden with a goal in the tenth minute, then sitting tight for the rest of that game and the entirety of the next two against Uruguay and Israel, to make sure of the two 0–0 draws they needed to top their group. The only time in the tournament when they had attacked was when they had to, in the previous round against Mexico, after going 1–0 down. Finding themselves needing to score two goals, they'd shown that they did possess flair after all by scoring four.

Against the Germans the *azzurri*'s first goal was rather fortunate. Boninsegna belted towards the German goal, ball at his feet, his momentum giving him the rub of the green in two challenges from German defenders. Arriving at the edge of the box he saw the chance for a snapshot, and his left-footer zipped past a startled Sepp Maier. This signalled the Italian defensive blanket to come down. The Germans were allowed all the space they wanted until they neared the Italian box, at which point things turned Piccadilly Circus at rush hour. Nevertheless Seeler, Grabowski and Overath all found themselves in positions from which they might well have scored with a little more composure. But there was something about the Germans and important World Cup matches in that era that seemed to give them super-human powers deep into injury time. Three minutes had passed beyond the ninety when winger Grabowski, who'd started a game for once after tormenting England's Terry Cooper as substitute in the quarter-final, pumped a ball into the box. Full-back Schnellinger, playing in his fourth World Cup, stole in to thump the ball home and push an otherwise ordinary game into the twilight zone.

Despite the psychological blow of such a late goal (and the even later Beckenbauer let-off), the game looked to be Italy's for the taking in extra-time, especially as German manager Helmut Schoen had used both substitutes early in the second half and his team was playing with a crippled sweeper and captain. But the Germans had become extra-time experts. And it looked like they'd stolen the tie for a place in the final when their new-found scoring sensation Gerd Muller, soon to be named European Footballer of the Year, ghosted between Albertosi and Poletti to pickpocket his ninth goal of the tournament five minutes into extra-time.

Then things really started to get interesting. In the ninety-ninth minute substitute Gianni 'golden boy' Rivera, who'd come on for Mazzola at half-time (the fact that Italy didn't want to play both of their world-class creative players at the same time was revealing), hit in a free kick and central defensive mugger-in-chief Tarcisio Burgnich, for once out of his own half and in his opponents' box, drilled home. Five minutes later Luigi 'rumble of thunder' Riva sent Italy wild with a stunning goal, beating Schnellinger with a Travolta twist and hitting the ball between keeper and post with a left-footed drive that may well have been intended as a cross. With five minutes to go, the Germans showed once more that their necks don't bend when times are hard, and Seeler, after having one header saved by the Italian keeper, nodded another across the goalmouth and the irrepressible Gerd Muller was there to hit home his second of the game, and tenth of the tournament. It was 3–3.

For a long time it had been evident that the match was going to be won by the team with more running in their legs, and Italian talisman Boninsegna proved that his were still full of go when he got to the German by-line straight from the restart, looked up to see Rivera free, laid back a perfect ball, and rejoiced when the Italian midfielder whumped it into the net. For once the Germans had no last-minute reply. Ecstatic Italy were in the final. That was big news, but not half as big as the fact that the most defensive team in the world had scored four (for the second time in a week) and let in three. They were to concede another four before the week was out.

6

England 3   Hungary 6
Friendly
Wembley Stadium, attendance 100,000
25 November 1953

'Look at that little fat chap there,' one England player is said to have chuckled as he spotted Ferenc Puskas in the Wembley tunnel. 'We'll murder this lot.' Whoever it was, it didn't take long for the Hungarians to wipe the smile off his face.

At a time when England had only recently started to bother entering the World Cup, until 1950 deemed insignificant by the FA, the founders of football were about to be taught a footballing lesson by Ferenc Puskas and his 'magnificent Magyars'. Inside a minute the England players, and their fans, were smiling no more as Hungarian striker Hidegkuti swerved skilfully on the edge of the box and fired the ball past Merrick in the England goal from twenty yards. Sixty seconds gone, 1–0 to Hungary, and history was in the making. Over the next eighty-nine minutes the speed of thought, movement off the ball and awesome striking power of the Hungarians made England, then considered the best team in the world and never before beaten on home soil by 'continental' opposition, look positively second-rate. The Hungarians played in a way Wembley had never

seen. With their pinpoint passing and seemingly tele-
pathic running off the ball, Hungary came to the home
of football and humiliated the landlords.

Tom Finney described the Hungarians as 'the finest
team ever to sort out the intricacies of this wonderful
game'. Between 1950 and 1956 the side, built around
the army team Honved, took the world by storm,
winning the Olympic title and reaching the 1954 World
Cup final only to be defeated 3–2 by Germany (a defeat
explained by many as due to over-confidence: the Hungarians were 2–0 up after just eight minutes). Before the
England game they had earned twenty wins in twenty-
three games. Still, nobody thought they'd win at
Wembley. Over the previous few years the warning signs
that the rest of the world was catching England up had
been there for all the world to see, but few were prepared
to accept the fact that England no longer ruled the
world. It took a short, chubby Hungarian to hammer
the message home.

With the left-footed Puskas running the show at
Wembley, Hungary seemed to be playing a different
game altogether. Puskas spearheaded the attack with the
tall, elegant Sando Kocsis, while Hidegkuti foraged
behind them. Time and time again the English defence
stood bewildered as the Hungarian strikeforce ran rings
around them. England were still in the game early in the
first half, however, Mortensen putting Sewell through
to equalize in the thirteenth minute. Three goals in seven
minutes from Hungary (including one from Puskas when
he dragged the ball back with his studs and then fired
in from a narrow angle) spelled the end of England's

chances and the end of an era in English football. The Hungarian demolition of England sent shockwaves through the English game. 'The New Wembley Wizards' screamed the morning paper headlines, 'Now It's Back To School For England'. *The Times* wrote: 'Yesterday the inevitable happened, England at last were beaten by the foreign invader.' In the post-mortem that followed the international playing careers of Alf Ramsey, Stan Mortensen, Harry Johnson and Bill Eckersley came to an abrupt end.

Despite fielding a strong side which included Sir Stanley Matthews and Billy Wright, England were bamboozled by the skill and movement of their Hungarian counterparts. By half-time the Magyars were 4–2 ahead with a display of continental artistry combined with British-style enterprise and vigour. Football legend has it that on the afternoon of the match a young Bobby Moore was delivering evening newspapers in London. When he saw the half-time score in the 'late news' section he dismissed it, knowing for sure that it must be a misprint. In the second half Ramsey converted a penalty but Hidegkuti completed his hat-trick at the other end. It finished 6–3 and the crowd was stunned. If the Hungarians hadn't seemingly eased off in the final twenty minutes or so the damage could have been even worse.

In 1956, in the wake of the Hungarian revolution, the team's reign as the greatest in world football came to a premature end. Puskas, who had scored an incredible eighty-three goals in eighty-four internationals, fled and was initially reported dead, before settling in Austria and then Spain. There he helped Real Madrid to European glory and even played four international games for his adopted homeland. His Real Madrid colleague Francisco Gento once said: 'His shooting was unbelievable and his left foot was like a hand, he could do anything with it. In the showers he would even juggle with the soap.'

Six months after the Wembley defeat, England (with seven changes) travelled to Budapest and this time it was a massacre: they were beaten 7–1. Fortunately for them, Puskas never played at Wembley again.

I was there . . . Sir Stanley Matthews

They were simply a great team and they took us apart. We knew they were a good side before the match but we were always confident, you always think you're going to win a match whoever you're playing. But the Hungarians really did teach us a thing or two that day. They were a fantastic side. Puskas got all the headlines but Hidegkuti was quite superb too. He played deep and nobody picked him up, and if you give a man with that much skill that much time then you're going to be in trouble. They had two great wingers as well and, of course, Puskas was a great player: he had an educated left foot. The goal he scored when he dragged the ball back and shot all in one movement was quite brilliant.

When you are on the pitch you aren't thinking about what the other team is doing, you're trying to get on with it yourself, so it was only afterwards that we appreciated their skill. After the match we were shocked. We were upset and disappointed to have lost, but they really had taught us a lesson. They were undoubtedly the best international team that I ever played against.

I was there . . . Ken Barber

It was standing on the Wembley terraces that remarkable day. Ever since England had been beaten by the USA in the World Cup in 1950, people had been wondering who would be the first team to beat them at Wembley, and many in the crowd were saying that this could be the day.

We had heard of Puskas and the papers had been saying that Hungary were a very good side, but no one really knew the team or what to expect. When the match started we couldn't believe what we were seeing, it was a totally different system to anything we'd seen before. We'd never seen a striker play so deep as Hidegkuti was doing. I think it was Henry Johnstone, the England centre-half, who complained afterwards: 'I had no one to mark.' Hidegkuti, Kocsis and Puskas played in the middle, but when players had the ball in that position we were used to seeing it played out to the wings where the winger would beat the full-back and get his cross in. What the Hungarians were doing was playing diagonal balls behind the full-backs towards the corner flag, where their wingers would run on to it and fire in their crosses with the England defence totally stranded. Of course you see this quite a lot nowadays, but we'd never seen anything like it before.

The reaction of the crowd was one of admiration, for the skill of the Hungarians and their tactics. Puskas was remembered mainly for that incredible goal he scored when he dragged the ball back and left Billy Wright floundering. Afterwards it was all the talk around football grounds for several months. People respected what they had seen, they were not downhearted, and there was certainly no talk of 'Winterbottom out' or anything like that. People thought that it was no disgrace to lose to such a good side, in fact I think some people were relieved that the unbeaten record had finally fallen to such a fantastic team.

7

France 3   West Germany 3
(a.e.t., 4–5 on penalties)
World Cup semi-final
Seville, attendance 63,000
7 July 1982

alk to any Frenchman about this match and they'll
spit the word 'injustice' right back in your face.
   In a match worthy of Pelé's description of 'the
beautiful game', it was a moment of brutal ugliness
which is remembered as the defining moment. With the
scores level at 1–1 in the second half, French substitute
Patrick Battiston raced clear to latch on to a superb
Platini pass. He had only been on the pitch for six
minutes when he was suddenly clean through with only
Schumacher in the German goal to beat. As Battiston
met the ball the German keeper met him. Schumacher
charged out of his box and leapt at Battiston, clattering
into him and seeming to strike his face with his forearm.
It was a sickening challenge that sent the Frenchman
flying and knocked him out cold, and the ball bobbled
weakly past the post. Initially there were fears for Battiston's life as the physios rushed to his aid, but after three
long minutes he was finally stretchered off and taken to
hospital. As he was carried away, still unconscious and
minus two teeth, Platini held his hand all the way to the
touchline. With yet another sub on for France, scandal-

ously the Germans were awarded a goal kick. Undoubtedly Schumacher should have been sent off but the Dutch referee said he didn't see the incident and his linesman, inexplicably, didn't enlighten him. The French were unsettled and a defender short, but what made the whole incident so galling was that the match went to penalties and it was Schumacher's saves which robbed France of their first-ever appearance in a World Cup final.

The match was an epic contest. Of all the games that supposedly 'had everything', this was one that truly did, with the dream football of the French finally overcome by the resilience of Germans after two and a half hours of gripping drama. West Germany opened the scoring in the eighteenth minute thanks to little striker Pierre Littbarski, who fired home after Fischer's shot rebounded off Ettori's knees. It was against the run of play. Up to the goal Giresse and Platini had been commanding the midfield, but within ten minutes France were level. Giresse played a clever free kick into the German box, creating turmoil, and when Bernd Forster fouled Rocheteau the referee pointed to the spot. Platini kissed the ball, stepped up, and the stadium erupted when he converted. It was 1–1 and that's how it stayed until Schumacher's assault, although after it the French were naturally unsettled and Ettori made two fine saves to keep them in it.

The first period of extra-time belonged to the French. First Tresor on ninety-three minutes and then Giresse four minutes later fired past the villainous Schumacher and that, it seemed, was that. In spite of the keeper's cynicism the team of Michel Platini and Alain Giresse –

the 'European Brazilians' – looked set to grace the final for the first time ever. With a footballing soul right off the beaches of Rio not the training camps of Europe, the French continued to press forward. But the Germans, with a semi-fit Karl-Heinz Rummenigge on as a last-ditch substitute, refused to accept defeat and in one of their famous World Cup revivals scored twice in five minutes. After Giresse's goal Rummenigge immediately began to ravage the French defence. After 102 minutes he met Littbarski's tap at the near post to make it 2–3. Then, just five minutes later, Hrubesch headed the ball back across goal and Fischer hooked it in over his left shoulder. It was 3–3 but the excitement wasn't over and French full-back Amoros nearly won it right at the death with a glorious thirty-yard shot which crashed against Schumacher's bar.

So it was penalties. First Giresse, then Kaltz, Amoros, Breitner and Rocheteau scored. But Stielike missed for West Germany. He was distraught, flinging himself to the ground in despair where he was consoled by Littbarski. Stielike couldn't watch as Didier Six stepped up next . . . but Schumacher saved. It was level yet again. Next Littbarski scored and so, of course, did Platini and Rummenigge. Up stepped Maxime Bossis, but his weak shot was comfortably saved by Schumacher. The injustice was complete and it just fell to Horst Hrubesch to shoot the West Germans into the final.

Afterwards the war of words began. French boss Hidalgo, normally a quiet man, furiously attacked the referee's weak performance. And, claiming he and Giresse had both been fouled before it, Platini described

Rummenigge's goal as 'scandalous'. Asked about the Schumacher incident, Hidalgo claimed: 'We have been eliminated brutally. I would say, scientifically.' The West Germans had earned themselves the mantle of most unpopular team in the tournament by crudely manufacturing a 1–0 win over their Austrian neighbours in the opening phase, a result which saw both teams go through. After this game they became just about the most unpopular World Cup finalists ever, and the whole of France was cheering along with the rest of the world when Italy beat them three days later in Madrid.

I was there . . . Martin Tyler

This game was the arch romantics against the arch realists, but it's a little unfair on West Germany that they are remembered as the party poopers. The Schumacher incident apart, the Germans made a huge contribution – they had as many chances as the French and what looked a perfectly good goal disallowed – and should have been applauded just as much as France. The French team was just beginning to develop into a winning side, but it was not quite there, and I think losing this match was one of the big lessons it learnt on the way to winning the European Championships in 1984. No team should let a 3–1 lead slip in extra-time. Of course the French midfield was something else: Tigana, Giresse and Platini were wonderful players. In fact, the French front players Rocheteau and Six did most of their work off the ball, moving defenders around to make space for these three.

Platini, however, had not yet moved to Italy and he wasn't yet at his peak as a player.

Both sides had their moments in the match and there were plenty of chances. If Amoros's shot had gone in instead of hitting the bar then we'd be looking at it in a totally different light. But I really think it's important not to minimize the part the Germans played in the match. The sour taste the match leaves in your mouth was left by one man and one man only, and it's incredible when you think what would happen to Schumacher now. I think he was probably saved by the fact that the ball looked like it might go in, and he clattered into Battiston while everyone was watching the ball. I think self-protection would be Schumacher's defence, but it was a disgraceful challenge which looks worse every time you see it. Let's face it, he should never have been around to save penalties in the shoot-out. It was the first penalty shoot-out ever in the World Cup finals and, as always, it seemed a terrible way to end such a contest. I remember at the time people were saying, 'Well, if they're out there for a couple of months what difference would an extra couple of days make?' But this was the beginning of a new era for World Cups, where TV and commercialism called the shots, and a penalty shoot-out it was.

The thing I remember about the shoot-out is little Pierre Littbarski. He was such an enthusiastic young man and a really nice bloke too, and when Stielike missed he was the only German who showed the compassion to console him. And in fact the TV cameras missed Schumacher saving Didier Six's penalty because the cameras were on them.

At the end of more than two hours of titanic struggle, it was the Germans who had finally won through. Everyone rightly remembers it for the flamboyant French coming oh-so-close to their first-ever World Cup final, but it couldn't have been such a classic if there was only one side contributing.

8

England 0   Brazil 1
World Cup qualifying round, group three
Guadalajara, Mexico, attendance 66,000
7 June 1970

'The greatest match I ever played in,' said the late, great Bobby Moore some years after his famous 'see you in the final' embrace with Pelé in the Guadalajara centre circle. To many, however, this was the final. The winners of the last three tournaments head to head in the World Cup for the first time since 1962. The free-flowing Brazilians against the mighty England, it was the match the world wanted to see. Played in ninety-eight-degree noon heat so as not to inconvenience European TV viewers (noon Mexico time is seven p.m. in the UK), every English player lost at least ten pounds in weight. Yet the match didn't disappoint. A rolling, strolling classic, with occasional bursts of speed and breathtaking skill, the game is remembered for Jairzinho's goal, Astle's miss, Moore's breathtaking defending and, of course, the greatest save of all time.

England's preparation for the game, their second in group three after beating Romania 1–0, was hardly ideal. The night before the match a crowd had gathered outside the team's hotel to partake in that most traditional of South American pre-match rituals, making loads of noise to keep the other team awake all night. On the street next to the hotel the crowd hooted car horns, banged drums and chanted 'Bra-zil' through the night and most of the England players were forced to switch rooms in the early hours. Though the chants were for the opposition, the crowd was as much anti-English as pro-Brazil. Sir Alf Ramsey, never the most sensitive of men, had managed single-handedly to upset the whole of Mexico, it seemed. He'd refused to bring any Spanish-speaking press officials on the trip, banned his players from speaking to journalists and offended his hosts by hiring Findus to supply the team's food, including ten cases of tomato ketchup. Even the England team bus had been shipped over from dear old Blighty.

Brazil's preparations had gone slightly more smoothly. They had qualified with a 100 per cent record in their South American qualifying group, scoring twenty-three goals in the process, and were desperate to erase the bitter memories of 1966 when Pelé had limped out and Brazil didn't even make the quarter-finals. Under new coach Mario Zagalo, star of the 1958 and 1962 Brazilian teams, they had the sniff of World Cup glory.

Of the 66,000 that turned up for the match, at least 65,000 were screaming for Brazil. But, seemingly oblivious to the temperature, it was England who started best, stroking the ball around neatly – in almost Brazilian fashion in fact – and creating a couple of half-chances for Ball and Charlton. In the eleventh minute, however, Brazil broke forward and the crowd nearly got what they had come for. Carlos Alberto played the ball to Jairzinho on the right and, with an awesome change of pace, he steamed past Terry Cooper, hit the by-line, and unleashed a fearsome cross to the far post. Pelé met it on the run, powered his header towards the bottom left-hand corner and the stadium rose to acclaim a goal . . . just as Gordon Banks threw himself across his goalmouth and somehow turned the ball over the bar as it bounced on the line. Pelé was already turning away with his arms raised when Banks reached the ball. The stadium was stunned.

Spurred on by their goalkeeper's heroics, England began to go on the attack themselves. Brazilian keeper Felix saved twice at the feet of Bobby Charlton and then Francis Lee had a glorious chance. Wright's threaded centre found him six yards out with the goal gaping in front of him, but Lee put his header straight into the keeper's hands. With Moore controlling the defence, anticipating everything, winning everything, the game became a footballing chess match, played almost at walking pace but interspersed with exhilarating bursts of speed and skill. Moore was superb. Timing his tackles to perfection and coming away with the ball seemingly glued to his feet, he oozed class, and Pelé later said it was the finest performance by a defender he'd ever seen. One moment in the first half summed up the England skipper's performance. Brazil had a free kick outside the box and Jairzinho lined up at the end of the England wall with Moore behind him. As Rivelino unleashed his thunderbolt Jairzinho stepped aside, only for Moore to kill it nonchalantly and then stride majestically upfield with the ball.

In the second half Brazil upped the pressure. And in

the fifty-ninth minute, the greatest central defender in the world was helpless as Brazil took the lead, Jairzinho firing in from Pelé's perfect lay-off after Tostão's pass had ricocheted cruelly through Moore's legs. It was 1–0 to Brazil and England were on the ropes. Ramsey took off Charlton and Lee and brought on Colin Bell and Jeff Astle, and it was the latter who was to squander England's best chance of the game. Everaldo, no doubt dreaming of an ice-cool glass of water, incredibly presented Astle with the ball right on the Brazilian penalty spot. With the time and space to tee up a shot, Astle screwed his shot past the post. Ouch. Surely this was England's last chance, but there was still time for Alan Ball to hit the bar from just outside the box.

When the final whistle blew the two teams embraced in mutual respect. It had been a classic encounter. For England it meant a tougher quarter-final but the prospect of the two sides meeting in the final remained. Unfortunately it never happened, though to many this match will always be the real final of 1970.

I was there . . . Alan Mullery

I watched this game on video about three years ago, the first time I'd ever seen it, and I hadn't realized what a great match it was. They played so well and we played so well. I watched it with Gordon Banks and neither of us had remembered what a truly outstanding match it was. Brazil were such a good side, probably the best national side there has ever been, and we outplayed them for long periods of the game. We outpassed them for long spells and we created three or four really good chances: no one else did that against them in the whole tournament. We were that close to beating them, and if we'd met them in the final we knew we could put up a very good show.

I can remember the heat. It was a hundred degrees in the shade, except that there wasn't any shade. And hardly any of us had any sleep thanks to the noise outside the hotel, horns, drums, you name it. At three o'clock in the morning we all had to ask to be moved to the seventeenth floor. It was real South American dirty tricks, the Mexicans all wanted Brazil to win, but I guess you've got to expect it when you go out there.

I only really remember three incidents in the game. I was always like that when we'd lost: all I can remember of the FA Cup final I played in for Fulham is West Ham's two goals, but I can remember every second of the match when I won it with Chelsea in 1967. I remember Banks's save, Jairzinho's goal and Astle's miss. The save was truly incredible. I was supposed to have been marking Pelé but, with Terry Cooper out of the game, beaten for pace by Jairzinho, we all moved across one man. But Jairzinho's cross was so good that it fell right on Pelé's head. Even when Pelé was in mid-air he was screaming 'goal'. He headed it with such power, there was no way Banks could get across to the ball, he never had a cat in hell's chance. When he got to it no one could believe what they'd seen. I just went over to him, patted him on the head and said, 'Why didn't you catch it?'

When they scored we were disappointed of course,

but no way did we think we were out of it. And when Jeff Astle had that chance we thought we were back in it, but it wasn't to be. Afterwards, although we were down, we knew we'd given them a good game and in many ways it made us even more confident about the rest of the tournament. Many years later Pelé told me that we were the only team in the competition that Brazil feared.

After the match I had to do a drugs test, but I'd lost so much fluid that I couldn't give a urine sample. I'd lost a stone in weight and I had to drink eight bottles of Coke before I could give them anything. Even then there was so little urine I had to top it up with tap water, and knowing what the Mexican water was like I was quite surprised I passed!

I was there . . . Gordon Banks

I still get excited when I see the save on TV, it's been shown so many times, and of course it's nice when people talk about it as the greatest save ever. I just remember the cross coming over from Jairzinho, and Pelé meeting it perfectly. I was still right in the middle of the goal. If I'd thought I couldn't get there though I wouldn't have dived, I knew I had a chance – and a goalie is never beaten until the ball's got past him – and fortunately I got to it. The ball was bouncing up anyway so when I got my hand to it, it naturally flicked up over the bar. I wouldn't say I actually turned it over the bar, it's more like it caught my hand and went over.

All in all, though, it was such a great game. Both

teams played so well, we changed our style to suit the conditions, keeping the ball and then trying to do something special in the last third just like them. If we'd met them in the final it would've been a cracker, and I reckon we might just have won it.

9

England 2   West Germany 3
(full-time score 2–2)
World Cup quarter-final
Guanajuato Stadium, Mexico, attendance 24,000
14 June 1970

A fine England side's dismissal from the 1970 World
Cup at the hands of bitter rivals West Germany is
often attributed to a dodgy bottle of Mexican beer,
a couple of strange second-half substitutions by Alf
Ramsey, and a mysteriously disallowed Geoff Hurst goal
in extra-time. But a good deal of credit must be given
to the Germans for coming back from the dead.

First the dodgy beer. Gordon Banks, fêted as the best
keeper in the world at the time, had drunk the evil fluid
a couple of days before the game and come down with
the complaint commonly known as Montezuma's
revenge. So poor Banks was in no state to squat, let
alone stand between the posts. He was replaced by Chelsea's Peter Bonetti, who'd been a sound understudy to
Banks in the preceding four years, only letting in one
goal in six England victories. Unfortunately Bonetti 'the
Cat', who hadn't played any competitive football since
the FA Cup final in April, was to live up to his nickname
with a howler of a game that must still give him
nightmares.

And it all started so well. With England in red and

West Germany in white, echoes of the 1966 World Cup final were deafening, especially with five men on each side still left from that match, although the altitude and searing heat made the conditions just slightly different from that London occasion four years earlier. England played a similar wingless system, 4–4–2 this time, with Charlton and Peters deeper than normal, and the ruse gave Alf Ramsey's men the early edge, although chances were few and far between in the first half-hour. Then Alan Mullery picked up the ball deep in midfield and, after swapping passes with Francis Lee, laid it out to Keith Newton on the right. He dipped in an angled cross and Mullery half-volleyed past Sepp Maier. 1–0. Full-back Newton was again the provider for England's second goal, just after the break, having received possession from the hard-working Hurst. This time he played his angled ball to the far post where Martin Peters, ten years ahead of his time and ten milliseconds quicker than the better-positioned Berti Vogts, knocked the ball in.

England, renowned for not giving away goals, appeared to have the game in their pocket. But when West Germany brought on the tricky winger Grabowski, who tormented Terry Cooper down the right, the balance swung. Grabowski's legs were fresh. Cooper, who'd been overlapping like crazy in Ramsey's wingless system, looked like his namesake the boxer after twelve rounds with Muhammad Ali. With more than twenty minutes still on the clock, Ramsey prepared to make a substitution, but before he could do it Beckenbauer ran the ball towards the England box, unleashed a shot,

Bonetti dived over it and suddenly West Germany were in with a shout. With the game at 2–1 Ramsey provoked the talking-point of the century by leaving the flagging Cooper on the pitch and instead replacing Bobby Charlton with Colin Bell, then substituting Martin Peters with Norman 'bites yer legs' Hunter, thus drastically changing the shape of England's midfield. He later revealed that he was trying to save Charlton's legs for the semi-final. He was to pay for his complacency.

Charlton had been man marking Beckenbauer just as he did in 1966, and had pretty much nullified the German skipper, despite his goal. But soon after Charlton departed the score was 2–2. Schnellinger's cross found Seeler, who could only graze the ball with his head. Bonetti, out of position, watched in horror, with the rest of the nation back home, as it looped over him and into the net. West Germany were rampant now, and had their chances to win it. But it remained 2–2 until the final whistle. It was extra-time then, just like Wembley four years before, but without Charlton and Peters in the heart of England's midfield. This time Ramsey, who must have realized he'd made a disastrous error in substituting his best players and then having to play extra-time without them, couldn't find the words to rally his troops as he had four years previously. At Wembley Hurst had been the extra-time hero, and this was just the time, you'd think, for him to score again. Remarkably enough he did, from a cross by Francis Lee who had got to the by-line and whipped in a perfect ball. But the referee, bizarrely, disallowed the effort. Video replays show no possible reason for the decision, but this time there was no Russian linesman. In the second period West Germany scored. And it was to count. Grabowski, having beaten the hapless Cooper for the umpteenth time, crossed, Lohr headed down, and Gerd Muller, unmarked in front of goal, volleyed home.

England came close after that, but not close enough. West Germany progressed to the semi-finals, and England were not to play in the World Cup finals again for another twelve years. The whole country was in shock. The only thing that raised the nation from its torpor was a general election a few days later. Harold 'England only win the World Cup under Labour governments' Wilson had hoped the timing would coincide with England's glorious defence of the Jules Rimet trophy, but with England going out to their arch rivals (and while wearing red) there was no hope . . . Labour lost a seven-point lead in the polls and the Tories came from behind to win the election.

I was there . . . Colin Bell

To be honest I don't remember that much of the match, it's a bit of a blur. A lot of players remember everything, every corner, every shot, but I don't. I've never seen the match since although I know it was an exciting game. The thing that sticks in my mind most of all is Seeler's header. That was the goal that changed everything. It just hit the back of his head and went in, he never meant it. If he'd tried to do it a million times he'd never have done it again.

I don't think that losing Gordon Banks made as much

difference as people said at the time, although I think if Peter Bonetti had known earlier that he was playing – he didn't know until the morning of the game – he would certainly have been more ready for the match mentally. People have also made a lot about the substitution when I came on for Bobby Charlton, but it would have been the same result. It still would've been 3–2. Players were getting fatigued and we had to bring on fresh legs. The heat and humidity were like nothing I've ever experienced. I've never been as fit as I was when I came back from Mexico, just from running around in that heat and at such an altitude. After a match you'd have players literally gasping for water.

We were all distraught after the West Germany game of course. It was the end of two years of effort. We'd been preparing for two years for this World Cup, we'd been on tour to South America the previous year, and now it was all over. All that time and effort for nothing. It could have been so different. We knew that we were the team Brazil feared and we'd already given them one good game. If we could have won our group then things would have been very different, but I always say it was fate. We were destined to lose 3–2.

10

Everton 4   Liverpool 4
(full-time score 3–3)
FA Cup fifth-round replay
Goodison Park, attendance 37,648
20 February 1991

The mother of all Merseyside derbies. No matter how many times Kenny Dalglish's Reds went ahead in this amazing fifth-round replay, the Toffees just kept coming back. Four times Liverpool took the lead, four times Everton equalized.

'It was the classic case of the boxer who keeps getting back no matter how many times he's floored,' recalls Jimmy Armfield, who found himself completely breathless in the Goodison Park press box while commentating on the match he describes as 'the most thrilling I've ever seen'. And the excitement was all too much for Kenny Dalglish. The following day he told the Liverpool board he was resigning as manager, and by the end of the week he'd cleared his desk and left Ronnie Moran in charge. The stress of managing the most successful club in England had taken its toll, and seeing Everton claw their way back into this match obviously hadn't done much for his blood pressure. 'It was incredible,' says Armfield. 'I just kept saying, "They can't possibly come back again", but they kept doing it. It was such an exhilarating game, everything that's good about English football was on show. Passion, pace, skill and commitment . . . and some great, great goals.'

At the time of the match Liverpool were sitting pretty at the top of the table while Everton were struggling. But the Toffeemen had earned a 1–1 draw at Anfield the previous Saturday, and with nearly 40,000 packing into Goodison Park the form book was thrown out of the window, but not until it had been ripped up, shredded and burnt to a cinder for good measure. Peter Beardsley got things started, picking up the pieces after Andy Hinchcliffe had cleared Ian Rush's header off the line, to make it 1–0, but Graeme Sharp levelled the scores just after half-time. With seventy-one minutes on the clock Beardsley took control on the edge of the Everton box and fired an unstoppable shot into the top corner, only for Graeme Sharp to equalize for a second time just a few minutes later, after Nicol and Grobbelaar had got in a tangle. This was a rip-roaring clash all right, one that was fast becoming a classic, and it wasn't level for long. As extra-time loomed, Ian Rush's near-post header put Liverpool back in front yet again and seemingly into the next round. Then along came Tony Cottee. When Rush's header hit the back of the net, Howard Kendall told Cottee to warm up.

After his £2m move to Goodison, things hadn't been going exactly to plan for the former West Ham striker and his relationship with Howard Kendall could not have been described as blossoming. But with six minutes to go Cottee was Kendall's last throw of the dice, and the Goodison crowd roared his arrival more in hope than expectation. Five minutes later the place erupted. With only his second touch of the match Cottee scored. He'd sprung off the bench and into Mersey legend with a deft flick of the right boot which sent the ball past Grobbelaar and most of the crowd into ecstasy.

Extra-time. By now the pace was relentless, serious end-to-end stuff. Then they did it again. This time it was John Barnes who put Liverpool back in front. After 102 furious minutes he curled an outrageous shot from the corner of the box ('I don't apologize for using the word magnificent, because that's what it is' – Andy Gray, Sky Sports) and this time it was surely all over. 'I remember looking at the Everton fans all around me and it was like a funeral,' recalls Jimmy Armfield, 'then a few minutes later it was pandemonium. They were jumping about, the place went mad. I remember looking along the row and there was a man just sitting there with tears in his eyes.' The man who'd loosened the tear ducts of Evertonians everywhere . . . Tony Cottee. With six minutes of extra-time left on the clock he'd done it again, this time slipping the ball through Bruce Grobbelaar's legs in delight. 'The match was so special,' says Armfield. 'The crowd was fantastic, the players played their hearts out, the goals were superb. I've been in football forty years but I've never seen a game like it.'

And the second replay? A dull 1–0 win for Everton.

I was there . . . Tony Cottee

People always say, 'What a great match that must have been to play in', but they forget that I only came on with six minutes of normal time left. Before I did come on, though, I remember that it was a cracking game to watch. I mean I enjoy watching games anyway, although of course it's frustrating sitting in the dugout, and this match was particularly frustrating. Liverpool just kept scoring, and every time we drew level they'd score again. You just had the feeling that they'd win it.

With about ten minutes to go I remember Howard Kendall telling me to warm up, and Liverpool were winning 3–2. Then he called me over and said, 'Right Tony, go on and get the equalizer.' I looked up at the clock and there were six minutes left, and I thought, 'Cheers Howard, what do you expect me to do?' At least I was fresh, though, so I thought I'd just try and get in the area and get some sort of shot in, anything. I touched the ball once, I think, before I scored. I think it was Neil McDonald who drilled it in, then it sort of bounced off the defenders to Stuart McCall who flicked it through and I was first to react. On TV it probably looks an easy chance but it's always hard to get into the rhythm of things when you first come on, but I was keyed up, I was ready for it, and I stuck it away. The crowd went mad.

I remember watching the highlights on BBC later and Barry Davies was waffling away, saying, 'I don't think Cottee's had a touch yet', and then it came through to me and he said, 'He might get one now!', so I guess it worked out well for his commentary too.

Then it was extra-time. Everyone else was shattered and I was just getting warmed up. We restarted, John Barnes scored, and they were ahead again. And I think at that stage we all thought, 'Ah well that's it.' It's always hard to recover from a goal in extra-time. But I got another chance thanks to a mix-up in the Liverpool defence. I think it was Glenn Hysen who should have just hoofed it out but I managed to read what he was doing, get to the ball and just nick it through Grobbelaar's legs. And Goodison Park went crazy all over again. Apart from my debuts for West Ham and Everton this was definitely the best game I've ever been involved in; I don't say played in because I wasn't on from the start. It's probably the best Merseyside derby there's ever been.

And, of course, the match was made even more significant because Kenny Dalglish resigned the next day. Who knows, if I hadn't scored maybe he wouldn't have resigned! Anyway we won the replay, but I don't recall that match with much fondness. I'd played the next League game after the 4–4, and scored, and then I was left on the bench for the second replay and didn't get on. You could say I wasn't best pleased.

11

AC Milan 4   Barcelona 0
European Cup final

Olympic Stadium, Athens, attendance 70,000
18 May 1994

Milan, who had just won their third successive Serie
A Scudetto, were not used to being cast in the
role of underdogs, but against a Barcelona team
including Romario and Stoichkov in attack, and with
their central defensive partnership of Baresi and Costa-
curta out suspended, not many punters were betting on
the trophy going to the *Rossoneri*, losing finalists the
previous year to the soon-to-be-disgraced Marseille.

What followed, however, was a Milanese demolition
job, and one of the best displays of teamwork the European game has ever seen. This was the end of an era for
the great side Cruyff had built for the Catalan giants,
based around the creative sweeping of Dutchman Ronald
Koeman. It was a side that echoed the tic-tac-toc one-
touch passing total football that Cruyff had played such
an inspirational part in creating with Holland in the mid-
1970s, but one that was about to be taught a footballing
lesson. On the day all the fluid passing movements came
from Milan, and much of the credit must go to their
French midfielder Marcel Desailly. With his tireless work
he destroyed Barcelona's rhythm, and thus their power,

cutting off the supply route to their celebrated international striking duo.

If Desailly was the force that put Barca on the back foot, Dejan Savicevic was the attacking force that capitalized to push them over, scoring once and setting up two other goals. The former Yugoslav international striker created Milan's first goal, breaking free on the right and laying the ball across for unmarked Daniele Massaro to score. He got the third himself, robbing Nadal and slamming a wonderful volley past a startled Zubizaretta just after the break, a strike which, effectively, killed the match. And, after a quick free kick, it was Savicevic's rebound off the post that Desailly hammered home to give the rout the scoreline it deserved. Milan's second goal was the best of the lot, with Massaro rounding off a fifteen-pass move with a fifteen-yard shot to knock the heart out of the Catalans. It was Milan's fifth European Cup victory, which put them above Liverpool in the roll of honour, just one place behind the mighty Real Madrid.

'This was the greatest performance by a club side I've ever seen,' said former Serie A centre-half Paul Elliott. 'Everyone said Milan were about to meet their match, but Barcelona were completely outplayed. Every Milan player was at the peak of his form, they kept the ball under pressure like no team I have ever seen. It was men against boys.'

12

Crystal Palace 4   Liverpool 3
(full-time score 3–3)
FA Cup semi-final
Villa Park, attendance 38,389
8 April 1990

Dad's Army might have been a thing of the past in 1990, but 'they don't like it up 'em' was never more appropriate than it was on 8 April 1990 when Crystal Palace bombed themselves into the FA Cup final. It was the first time both FA Cup semis had been tele-vised live, and Palace and Liverpool dished up a lunchtime treat for the nation.

After fourteen minutes, however, you'd have thought Palace had about as much chance of making it to Wembley as, er, Geoff Thomas being called up for England. When Ian Rush put the Reds (playing in that fetching silver strip) 1–0 up, a repeat of the 9–0 thrashing Palace had suffered at Anfield earlier in the same season was on the cards. Rush latched on to a through-ball from John Barnes and coolly tucked it past Nigel Martyn. The Liverpool players hardly celebrated, it was as if they were going through the motions in the spring sunshine. This was their third FA Cup semi-final in succession and they'd not lost . . . yet.

Despite losing the lead, Palace, without the injured Ian Wright, comfortably held their own in the first half.

63

OK they didn't exactly look like ripping the Liverpool defence to shreds, but the shiny silver men from Anfield weren't doing that to them either. Then, come the second half, Palace, and the match, exploded into life.

Right from the kick-off John Pemberton, a man not known for sudden bursts of complete and utter insanity, totally lost his head. Neglecting all defensive duties he launched himself into a manic sixty-yard run down the left wing, surging past the Liverpool defence and crossing the ball into the box. Pandemonium. With the defence all over the place the ball fell to Mark Bright who deliriously volleyed home. It was 1–1, and suddenly a very different game altogether. Now it was all Palace. The Liverpool defence was rattling like Clive Dunn's kneecaps as the Palace mortar squad launched everything into the box. Every time the ball came anywhere near the Liverpool box it was panic stations, and on sixty-nine minutes the aerial bombardment paid dividends again. Gary O'Reilly, completely unmarked, headed Palace into a 2–1 lead. You could hear the sound of jaws dropping from Stanley Park to Selhurst. What was this? The mighty Liverpool being bundled out of the match by a bunch of upstarts from South London whom they'd already beaten 9–0 that season?

The Merseysiders rallied and suddenly it was the Palace defence under pressure. McMahon scored a monstrous volley with nine minutes to go, and when John Barnes slipped his penalty home two minutes later that, it seemed, was that. But two minutes from time Pemberton launched yet another high ball into the box, all hell broke loose and Andy Gray bundled the ball in to send one corner of the ground into utter mayhem.

Extra-time, and half the population needed five minutes' rest along with the players. There was more excitement to come, though. With the clock ticking down and a replay looming, Palace did it again. Another cross, this time a corner, yet more bedlam and Alan Pardew's head. 4–3. When the final whistle blew Steve Coppell jumped out of the dugout and punched the air in delight. Then he quickly looked round to make sure no one had seen him and slipped quietly back into the dressing-room.

I was there . . . Alan Smith (Palace assistant manager)

Our only game plan was to try and contain Liverpool. They'd already beaten us 9–0 and we didn't want another thrashing, especially with the whole country watching. We decided to play much deeper, to keep it tight, and hope that maybe we could nick something from a set-piece in the last twenty minutes.

In the first half we could have been four down. They were strolling it. They were passing round us, but they were so casual. It was almost as if they thought they could beat us at any time. So really we were happy that it was only 1–0 at half-time. Then, straight from the kick-off, John Pemberton went on his famous run. He completely disobeyed all our instructions. He'd been specifically told not to cross the halfway line. I didn't really see it because we were still coming out of the tunnel, but suddenly it was 1–1 and they were starting to panic.

It shocked them, that's for sure. I think they thought they were going to breeze it but as soon as we started putting their defence under pressure they were panicking. Psychologically I don't think they were prepared for it, they certainly didn't expect it. It was like everything was geared for attack and they couldn't defend properly. They were fine from open play but as soon as we got a set-piece situation they were all over the place. I mean, Gary O'Reilly was completely unmarked for his goal. It was incredible.

We tried to get the players to stick to the gameplan, containing them, and at 2–1 I thought we'd won it. Then they got a couple and it looked like they'd won it. When we scored again and the game went to extra-time I still felt that they would win it. Then Alan Pardew scored, he was completely unmarked again, and I thought, 'My God they've made another mistake.' I couldn't believe it.

Afterwards the feeling in the dressing-room was more a feeling of disbelief than jubilation. I remember going back to the dressing-room and the kit man was in tears and Steve Coppell and I just sat in the bath, stunned, trying to take it all in. Had this really happened?

13

Liverpool 5   Nottingham Forest 0
League Division One
Anfield, attendance 39,535
13 April 1988

om Finney called it an exhibition of football 'that'll never be bettered' and an awe-struck John Motson described it as 'football that nowhere in the world would you see better'. It finished Liverpool 5 Nottingham Forest 0, it could have been ten, it could have been fifteen. This was arguably the last great Liverpool side at its peak. Individually brilliant, collectively extraordinary. With Peter Beardsley running the show like a man possessed, every move was intricately crafted yet everything happened at such a breathtaking pace. Every time a player in a red shirt had the ball it looked a certain goal. This was one-touch, passing football with a cutting edge that didn't just slit open the Forest defence but sliced it into a thousand pieces. Five goals went in but the scoreline truly flattered Brian Clough's Forest who, though they continued to try to play Liverpool at their own game, were annihilated.

It went something like this: Houghton collects the ball from Hansen, beats two men, plays a one-two with Barnes which leaves him clean through. He makes no mistake with the finish. 1–0. Beardsley plays a thirty-

yard pass ('One of the best passes you'll ever see,' said
Motson) to put Aldridge clear, and the Irishman instinctively finds goal. 2–0. In the second half central defender
Gary Gillespie rounds off 'another bewildering piece of
Liverpool football' (thanks again, Motty) with a finish
Ian Rush would have been proud of from eight yards.
3–0. John Barnes beats his marker, reaches the by-line,
cuts it back to Beardsley who fires low and hard into the
bottom corner. 4–0. Beardsley plays it to Spackman on
the edge of the box who turns, takes two defenders with
him, squares the ball and Aldridge does the rest. 5–0.

It was fast, it was precise, it was vintage Liverpool.
From the build-up to the finishing, from the commitment to the creativity, it was a faultless performance.
'One of the finest exhibitions of football I've ever seen
in my life,' said Tom Finney afterwards. Forest had been
destroyed by the sort of football Anfield was coming to
expect from Kenny Dalglish's Barnes- and Beardsley-
inspired team, yet they'd never seen it played to perfection for a full ninety minutes before.

Liverpool duly won the League title and the Double
looked a mere formality. All they had to do was beat First
Division upstarts Wimbledon at Wembley, and there's no
way a team who could produce a performance like this
would lose to that lot . . .

I was there . . . Tom Finney

I've seen a few games in my time, and I've played in a
few as well, but I can honestly say that this is the best

League performance I've ever seen by any team, anywhere.

I was at Anfield that night because I was doing some work for the Football Trust and you couldn't have wished for more from a team. It was pure Liverpool, pure perfection. The team gelled together perfectly. They didn't just create chances, they finished them off without mercy, and you have to remember what a good side Forest were at the time as well. I remember saying what a brilliant performance it was afterwards and Bob Paisley said to me, 'Come on Tom, you're going a bit over the top aren't you?' But that's my opinion and I still stick by it.

14

Brazil 1   France 1
(a.e.t., 3–4 on penalties)
World Cup quarter-final
Guadalajara, Mexico, attendance 65,000
21 June 1986

The Brazil of Socrates, Zico and Careca against the France of Platini, Giresse and Tigana. A mouth-watering prospect and for once a classic on paper which didn't lose anything in translation. The only thing wrong with this match was that it had to be decided on penalties. In the Guadalajara cauldron, scene of so many great World Cup struggles, two great sides fought out end-to-end drama with a twist in the tail and a breath-taking, if ultimately unsatisfactory, finale.

But it was a finale which would never have taken place if Brazilian legend Zico, he of the deadly left foot, hadn't decided to take a penalty seventeen minutes from the end with his right. It was the decisive moment of the match. The kick wasn't good enough and French keeper Bats dived to his left to keep it out. Until then the Brazilians had been dominant and the French were lucky still to be in the game. Moving with the grace and power we'd come to expect from those wearing the famous yellow and green shirts, it looked like Brazil were toying with the French and were capable of winning the match whenever it took their fancy.

Socrates, the Brazilian midfield general, had been running the show majestically as always. In the early stages of the match his team had torn into the French. After fifteen minutes Socrates forced Bats into action with a rasping shot that the French keeper could only beat out. It was one-way traffic and Careca, who'd already scored four goals in the tournament, was giving the blue-shirted defence – the weak link in the great French side – a torrid time. After eighteen minutes the crumbling French defences finally cracked. Muller, the nippy winger, combined neatly with Junior on the edge of the box and Careca nonchalantly slipped Junior's pass into the net. It was 1–0 but it could have been three or four in the first half-hour; indeed Muller hit the post minutes after the goal.

Just before half-time, France were quite unexpectedly level when the great Michel Platini, celebrating his birthday, scored the equalizer. Attacking full-back Amoros slipped the ball to the dynamic Alain Giresse, who played in Dominic Rocheteau. His speculative cross took a deflection and found its way to Platini at the far post, and *le nombre dix* made no mistake. What a time to score, and France were back in a game they should already have lost. They were revitalized and the second half was an altogether different story. As the players tired the game developed into a titanic, super-skilful struggle, surging deliciously from one end of the field to the other. Bats was forced into more action, saving twice from Junior as well as Zico and the tiring Socrates. France had their chances too as the pendulum swung repeatedly, but when Bats brought down Branco and the referee pointed to the penalty spot it looked as if we were going to have a winner. Then Zico missed.

In extra-time, with the Brazilian coach deciding to leave Socrates on when he was clearly struggling in the heat, France had their best chances to win. Now it was the turn of Carlos in the Brazilian goal to keep his side in the tournament, saving well from Tigana and Bossis. One short spell in the final seconds summed this dazzling match up. In a single hold-yer-breath minute right at the end of extra-time the French striker Bellone zipped into the clear and appeared to be felled by Carlos, but before the cries for a penalty died down Socrates hit the bar at the other end. Calling this game dramatic would be like calling Shakespeare a good playwright.

For this game to go to penalties was a tragedy, and it was a tragedy for Brazil and their thousands of colourful fans in the stadium when Socrates and Cesar missed to send France through. A match to remember, another shoot-out ending to forget.

15

Celtic 2   Inter Milan 1
European Cup final
National Stadium, Lisbon, attendance 55,000
25 May 1967

Real Madrid, Benfica, AC Milan, Inter . . . and now Celtic. At last a British side had won the most famous club trophy in the world, the European Cup, and in some style. This was a victory for attacking football as well as a victory for Glasgow Celtic Football Club.

European football at the time was dominated by defensive tactics, and Helenio Herrera's Inter were the pioneers of *catenaccio*, and its most accomplished proponents. A team littered with internationals who had won the trophy in 1964 and 1965, Inter were the most sophisticated side in the world and masters at gaining a 1–0 lead and then holding out until the final whistle. But they'd never faced a team like this. Under Jock Stein, Celtic had only one tactic: out-and-out attack.

In the run-up to the final, Stein did everything he could to relax his players and exploit the camaraderie he'd built up. While the Italians were locked away in a secret hideaway, kept away from visitors and hangers-on, Stein booked Celtic into a plush hotel, made sure the doors were open to all and personally made sure the party never stopped. When the Celtic players emerged into the tunnel in Lisbon's National Stadium, to the bemusement of the Inter players they were bellowing out the Celtic song at the tops of their voices. Out on the pitch, Stein purposely sat on the bench earmarked for the great Herrera and refused to budge. The legendary Italian coach was apparently furious, but Stein would not give way and the Celtic players thought this was hilarious. No one was going to push Celtic around.

This was the season Celtic won everything they entered (doing a domestic treble and scoring 200 goals along the way), but after eight minutes of the final against Inter they were behind to a Mazzola penalty. Scoring one goal against this team was hard enough, getting two was going to be nigh on impossible, and after the goal Inter promptly and predictably shut up shop. But roared on by 12,000 travelling fans (accompanied by hundreds of enormous green shamrocks), Celtic began a barrage of the Inter goal. The score was still 1–0 at half-time but Stein urged his players to stick to their attacking principles and ordered them to shoot on sight.

In the second half the hooped shirts swarmed forward against the massed ranks of the Inter defence. But despite their brave efforts, it looked like it wasn't to be. First Bertie Auld hit the bar and then Tommy Gemmell rattled the woodwork, but *catenaccio* was holding out. Then, in the sixty-third minute, Celtic's pressure paid off. Bobby Murdoch picked up Gemmell's pass, switched to Jim Craig on the right wing, and his centre found Gemmell on the edge of the box. The left-back looked up and thundered his shot past Sarti in the Inter goal from twenty yards. The green and white army in the tree-lined ground went mad, but the best was yet to come. With seven minutes left and the match heading for an extra half-hour, Celtic scored again. Again Gemmell was at the heart of it. His pass from the left wing found Murdoch who blasted his shot in towards goal, but before it got there it cannoned off Steve Chalmers and into the back of the net. Goal!

Celtic had beaten Inter, Scotland had beaten Italy, Stein had outfoxed Herrera and Britain had its first-ever European champions. The Lisbon Lions roared their way into the history books in truly magnificent style. 'It was such a breakthrough,' recalls veteran commentator Archie McPherson. 'It was the end of an era and the end of Herrera, and it proved that *catenaccio* could be beaten by fresh legs and an attacking attitude. It was a fantastic night.'

The 1967 European Cup final triumph was Jock Stein's finest hour as Celtic boss, but by no means his only one. Metaphorically speaking the biggest 'big man' of them all, Stein pushed the Bhoys to nine Scottish titles in succession (ten altogether) plus eight Scottish Cups and six Scottish League Cups. But that night in Lisbon in 1967 was surely his finest hour.

I was there . . . Jim Craig

Throughout the build-up to the game I think we all felt we were going to win, it was like everything was going right for us.

Jock Stein was brilliant at getting the boys relaxed. The day before the match we turned up to train at the stadium and Inter were just coming off the pitch, and they stayed around to watch. Because they were watching us we just did a quick run through and then had a practice match, only Jock switched everyone's positions round to confuse them. The defenders were playing up front and the midfielders at the back, it was hilarious, but the Inter players must have thought our defence was a bit small. Then, the night before the game we went out to watch a match on TV. I think England were playing, and on the way back to the hotel we took a short-cut. This just shows how naive we were: we went down a pitch-dark alley, there could have been anything down there, broken glass or anything, and climbed over a wall into the hotel grounds. This was on the eve of a European Cup final!

We never had time to get nervous before the game because we had the only bus driver in Portugal who didn't know the way to the National Stadium, I mean can you believe it? We didn't even have a team talk but I think it all helped. None of us was worried about the game. We went into the tunnel singing the Celtic song, and there were these grim Italians in their blue and black stripes. When we got out on to the pitch we lined up, and Jimmy Johnstone turned to their left-back Facchetti, who was also the Italian left-back, and said, 'Hey big man, how about swapping jerseys after?' This guy just looked like he was thinking, 'What's going on?'

We just had this feeling that it was going to be our cup. We always felt our attacking system was suited to playing their defensive one, in fact I think an attacking team would have given us more problems. Even when some idiot called Craig brought an Inter player down in the box and the ref gave a penalty, none of our heads went down. I was just worried about what my dad would be thinking, because he was in the stands and it'd taken me ages to persuade him to fly out. He thought Inter would be too strong for us. Afterwards he just said to me, 'You jammy sod.' But the thing is, I misheard Jock Stein's instructions. When he said, 'Go out there and make a game of it,' I thought he said, 'Go out there and give them a goal start.'

It was a strange game in many ways in that most of the openings we made came from the full-backs, myself and Bobby Murdoch. The attackers' main role was to take the defence out of the way. It was unusual because in those days many full-backs never crossed the halfway line. My schoolteacher would have been horrified; I remember whenever I charged forward in a school game he'd bellow at me to get back.

After we'd won the match it was all a bit anti-climactic for us. The fans came on the pitch to celebrate which meant that we never got to do a lap of honour. There was no real presentation of the Cup to speak of, Billy McNeill had to fight his way through the crowd on his own to get it. We eventually got our medals at the banquet after the game, after the Italians had kept us waiting for two hours, when Billy came round with a shoebox and we all had to pick one out. So the day ended on a bit of a sad note really. Still, the reception we got when we returned to Glasgow made up for it.

16

Liverpool 0   Arsenal 2
League Division One
Anfield, attendance 41,783
26 May 1989

Try as Sky TV might, they will never engineer a championship finale like this one. But when Michael Thomas flicked the ball past Bruce Grobbelaar and somersaulted himself into the history books it was a once-in-a-lifetime, never-to-be-repeated moment that even people who hate Arsenal will never forget.

A few months before, Arsenal's young team looked to have the title sewn up. After soaring into a seemingly unassailable lead by February, they stuttered nervously to the finish while reigning champions Liverpool, ominously, clicked into a twenty-four-match unbeaten run. With away wins at Anfield about as common as Arsenal wins by any other score than 1–0, a two-goal victory was not exactly on the cards. But that's precisely what the Gunners needed on the final match of the season to wrench the title from the clutches of the then mighty Reds. An impossible task? George Graham didn't think so, although even he surely couldn't have anticipated Liverpool's negative tactics. Was the pressure too much? In the wake of Hillsborough this was Liverpool's third game in six days, including an FA Cup final, but with the Double at stake the fatigue, if there was any, can only have been mental.

In a show of post-Hillsborough support, the Arsenal players ran out with bouquets to present to the Liverpool crowd. But with the sounding of the referee's whistle, so went the Gunners' compassion. At half-time it was 0–0. Arsenal worked hard but hadn't really threatened. Liverpool appeared content to see out the match rather than win it to make sure. Arsenal still had a mountain to climb.

That all changed on fifty-two minutes. Set-piece specialists Adams and Bould went forward for a free kick on the edge of the box and Adams's presence unsettled the Liverpool defence, freeing Alan Smith to ghost in and glance Winterburn's cross into the corner. Four thousand Arsenal fans in a corner of Anfield were delirious. Suddenly the title was back within reach. This was getting very interesting.

Interesting, yes, but Liverpool calmly defended as the minutes ticked away. The inevitable Liverpool title was, surely, er, inevitable. 'One minute,' mouthed Steve McMahon to his team-mates as the Kop started to roar songs of celebration. A brave effort from Arsenal, it seemed, but the trophy was staying put.

Then it happened. In injury time. Last throw of the dice . . . John Lukic threw the ball to Lee Dixon, whose long pass was controlled by Smith, who hooked towards goal. Michael Thomas was suddenly one-on-one with Grobbelaar and 40,000 onlookers held their breath. With probably the coolest head in Britain, never mind the stadium, Thomas flicked the ball over Grobbelaar.

2–0. The championship was decided in the very last seconds of the season.

I was there . . . Alan Smith

George Graham was very confident that we could do it. I remember it was all very calm in the dressing-room before the game. He said that if we could keep a clean sheet until half-time and then sneak a goal in the second half we'd be in with a shout.

All I remember about my goal is that Tony Adams went for it and just missed it, and I just got the faintest touch, just a glance. The Liverpool players were appealing because it was an indirect free kick and they didn't think I'd got a touch, but I definitely did.

After we scored we never panicked, there was never any pressure on us. Even when the crowd was whistling we didn't really throw men forward. At that time, if we were losing a game, often one of the centre-halves would go up front. But even with a few minutes left we didn't do any of that, and I always thought we'd score again. I didn't really know how late in the day it was when Michael Thomas scored, but I remember the crowd whistling, and when he did it was just amazing.

When the final whistle went it was an incredible feeling, and it was some atmosphere in the dressing-room. We got a great reception from the Liverpool crowd and the people at Anfield were great as well, there were no sour grapes.

17

Blackpool 4   Bolton 3
FA Cup final
Wembley Stadium, attendance 100,000
2 May 1953

espite Stan Mortensen's hat-trick, this was only ever
going to be 'the Matthews final'. Stanley Matthews.
Footballing legend, national hero and, at last, FA
Cup winner. But only just, and only after one of the
most thrilling Cup finals on record.

It had a fairy-tale ending all right, but for most of the
match it seemed that the Wanderers simply hadn't read
the script. Apart from the people of Bolton, the entire
nation was gunning for Matthews's Blackpool. It was
Coronation year and the country wanted a final to
provide a fitting celebration, and that meant a winner's
medal for thirty-eight-year-old Matthews. But with
twenty minutes to go they were 1–3 down to a Bolton
team inspired by Nat Lofthouse. They came to spoil the
party and were making a pretty good job of it.

Up to the seventieth minute Matthews, who'd nearly
failed to make the team after pulling a muscle in training
a few days before, wasn't having the greatest of games,
in fact he had a relatively poor first half. But the 'wizard
of dribble' wasn't beaten yet. Charging down the right
wing he curled in a cross, Bolton keeper Stan Hanson

could only get his fingertips to it and Stan Mortensen slid in to make it 2–3. Suddenly Matthews was alive. With the majority of the crowd and the entire country willing Blackpool back into it, he began to show flashes of his magic, bamboozling the Bolton defence with his trickery. But with three minutes to go it was still 2–3. Then Blackpool got a free kick outside the area and Mortensen, the man with the hardest shot in football, had a pop. Instantly Blackpool were level at 3–3.

With Bolton shell-shocked, Blackpool were straight at them again from the kick-off with Matthews clapping his hands and urging his team-mates forward. Straight away Bolton lost possession and the ball found its way to Matthews on the wing. Cutting towards goal he drew half the defence, Stan Mortensen took what was left of it with him, and Matthews squared the ball to Bill Perry who fired straight into the bottom left-hand corner of the goal. The crowd went wild. After the game Matthews was lifted shoulder-high by his colleagues and paraded around a jubilant Wembley.

'The 1953 Cup final was my most unforgettable match,' Sir Stanley said years later. 'But I did not win the game on my own. That's a myth. It was a great team effort.' Apart from Bolton the only loser was Mortensen, the man who scored a hat-trick in a match named after someone else. But if Bolton didn't even mind losing, it's unlikely he did. As Nat Lofthouse said: 'When it was all over, I felt it couldn't have gone to a better man. There were no recriminations in our dressing-room. I don't think a bullet would have stopped Stan in the last seventeen minutes.'

I was there . . . Jimmy Armfield

The Blackpool v. Bolton final was what made me decide to become a professional footballer. I was a seventeen-year-old Blackpool reserve at the time but I'd just passed my A levels so I had the opportunity to go to university if I wanted to. I went to the match with the rest of the reserve players and club officials and afterwards I decided that I had to try and make it in the game. I'm not easily swayed, but this match pushed me over the edge, and I've never regretted it. It was such an emotional day. The country was coming out of a difficult period, after the war and rationing and everything. TV had just started to come on the scene and anyone who had a set had 10,000 neighbours round that day. The whole nation wanted Stanley Matthews to win, he was a national institution and a football genius and it was deemed that he should have an FA Cup winner's medal.

It was one of those years. Gordon Richards won the Derby, Everest was conquered . . . it was a year of heroes and Stanley Matthews fitted the bill. He was different. He made you stop and look at him, he was magnetic. On the field he was merciless, he was ultra-professional. He was so skilful but he was also incredibly fit. I can honestly say that I never saw him out of breath. But as well as his footballing talent, people also loved him for his humility.

As for the match, well, fate didn't smile on Bolton; everyone outside Bolton wanted Blackpool. The match itself was like it had been written to a script. 3–1 down with so little time to go, only a miracle could see

Blackpool through, but two goals from Stan Mortensen turned the game upside down. The second was a free kick, and I'd never seen him take a free kick before in my life. He said he saw a hole in the wall and just blasted it.

From then on Bolton knew they couldn't win. They called Matthews the 'wizard of dribble' but he was much more than that. He made the winning goal and I can remember just standing there in the crowd, with all the Blackpool people, cheering and clapping. It was like delirium. Although I can remember feeling sorry for Bolton, there's no way they could have won that day.

18

Liverpool 3   St Etienne 1
European Cup quarter-final, second leg
Anfield, attendance 55,043
17 March 1977

With their bright green shirts and fluid attacking football, St Etienne were the darlings of European football at the beginning of 1977. But by the end of the year it was the name of Liverpool that struck fear into the hearts of European coaches. And if any one match symbolizes that glorious era, those misty nights at Anfield with the Kop packed to bursting point, it is this one, with pulsating attacking football from both sides making it truly a night to remember.

A goal down from the first leg, the crowd erupted when Keegan lobbed the home side ahead on the night and level in the tie. With the French supporters chanting their famous refrain 'Allez les Verts', St Etienne powered forward time and time again and Ray Clemence demonstrated his full acrobatics repertoire to keep the score at 1–0.

Six minutes into the second half, Bathenay put St Etienne in front on aggregate and, for a few seconds at least, Anfield went silent. It didn't last long though, with the bilingual Kop roaring 'Allez les Rouges' as the men in red charged forward. Ray Kennedy made it 2–1 on

85

the night and 2–2 on aggregate with one of his trade-mark strikes from the edge of the box. But it wasn't enough. Liverpool had to go for broke thanks to the away goals rule.

In the seventy-second minute John Toshack was forced to limp off and on came ginger-topped super-sub David Fairclough. Described rather unfairly in *The Official History of Liverpool* as 'the spindly legged youth', Fairclough was about to experience his finest moment in football. Collecting a pass from Ray Kennedy he ran at the French defence, sprinting forty yards, swerving past two defenders and planting the ball home right in front of the Kop. The roar was so loud they probably heard it on the other side of the Channel.

'No one had a clue what David was doing,' recalls Emlyn Hughes, 'because he didn't know himself. We were going, "Pass it David, pass it . . . keep going David, keep going . . . shoot. Yessss." It was fantastic. It was the greatest game of my career. The atmosphere, the fervour, everything. People at the club always used to tell us about the great European nights in the 1960s, but this must have equalled any of those.

'The thing is St Etienne were a really, really good side. But with the whole of Anfield willing the ball in we played some super stuff, and as soon as the ball went in for David's goal I just knew we were going to win the European Cup.'

I was there . . . David Fairclough

I can recall that night so vividly, even without looking at the video . . . mind you I've got copies of it all over the house just in case any of them get wiped off.

We always knew we were in for a big tie when we drew St Etienne. They were the team of the moment and they'd been unlucky to lose the final the year before to Bayern Munich, and they'd kept the team together. They were a great side, and we were pleased to come away from the first leg with just a 1–0 defeat.

When we arrived in the coach at Anfield for the second leg the weight of people in the streets around the ground was incredible. The match had really captured the imagination and there were thousands of French fans too, wearing these luminous green permed wigs. I've never seen as many flags on the Kop as there were that night. The sound was unreal as we came out of the tunnel, there was no escape from it, you were trapped. It was so loud, much louder than anything you hear now. I was really nervous just sitting in the dugout, scared of going on really. I remember saying to Brian Kettle, who was one of the other subs, 'Imagine going on in this?'

The match started but after just a few minutes Kevin Keegan scored. I think it was a bit of a fluke actually, the wind caught it and carried it over the keeper's head, and we were level. At half-time the subs were sent out to warm up on the pitch, which was unusual. I think it was just to prepare us for the unique atmosphere. I just tried to make sure that I didn't trip over my own feet.

In the second half Bathenay scored and, to be honest, we looked out of it. To score two goals against this side looked impossible and the feeling on the bench was, 'We're not going to do this.' I was just about to come on when Ray Kennedy made it 2–2 on aggregate. Bob Paisley took John Toshack off and said to me: 'Go on and roam around, just try and grab a piece of something.' I had a free role.

Anyway, with about six minutes to go Ray Kennedy had the ball, and he always used to say to me, 'If I've got the ball and I'm running into trouble, I'll just lift it beyond the centre-backs, so look out for that.' I thought that's what he might do, so I was ready when the ball came over the top and then it was a fifty-fifty between me and Lopez. I managed to shrug him off and then came across him and I was bearing down on goal right in front of the Kop. I was right in the centre of the goal and I knew there were a couple of defenders bearing down on me. I just thought, 'Get it on target.' Bob Paisley always used to say, 'Hit it close to the keeper and he won't be able to get down to it', which is what I tried to do, and as soon as I hit it I knew it was in.

Then I set off on a run round the ground, but Jimmy Case stopped me and the next thing I knew all the lads were on top of me. I remember Kevin Keegan saying in my ear, 'Stay down, stay down, use up some time.' By the time I got back to the halfway line I was completely exhausted, I'd used up all my energy in the celebrations, and the noise was unbelievable. Afterwards the lads wanted to swap shirts because they'd never seen anything like these green shirts, but I couldn't have swapped mine and I've still got it. In fact I was showing it to my son the other night and he said, 'Wow, I'm touching history.' It's nice to have it.

That night I just went home and watched the match on the telly. I was with a mate and on the way back we stopped off at the local pub. But when we got to the door we looked at our watches and it was nearly ten thirty, we thought we'd never get a drink so we went home. Afterwards I told another mate this and he said, 'What do you mean you wouldn't have got a drink, Liverpool was yours that night, you could've had anything you wanted.'

19

Tottenham 3   Manchester City 2
FA Cup final replay
Wembley Stadium, attendance 92,000
14 May 1981

icardo Villa, the second most miserable man in the
stadium in the first match of the 100th FA Cup
final, was probably the happiest man in the world
after the replay.

Big, bearded Villa, ineffective in the first game, was
substituted halfway through the second half for young
Gary Brooke, with Spurs 1–0 down to a Tommy Hutchison goal. As he trudged off the pitch in tears, he turned
to look at the outcome of a Spurs free kick. Hoddle's
thumped curler hit Hutchison on the shoulder, drifted
past a recumbent Joe Corrigan, and Spurs forced a replay.
Manager Keith Burkinshaw decided to keep faith in Villa
for the replay, and it was one of the best decisions he
ever made. Not only did the Argentinian midfielder give
Spurs the lead, belting a loose ball home early on after
Ardiles and Archibald's shots had been blocked and
parried, he also scored one of the best goals Wembley has
ever seen to give Spurs their seventh Cup win. Thirteen
minutes remained with the score at 2–2 when Villa
received a short pass on the left from Irish international
Tony Galvin. Big Ricky had one thing on his mind, and

his single-minded drive for goal saw him twist and turn past Tommy Caton three times, Ray Ranson twice and Nicky Reid before, almost magically, drawing Corrigan and shooting under his dive. It was a fitting climax to the 100th final.

Manchester City had overturned Villa's seventh-minute opener with a whistling volley from young Steve MacKenzie on ten minutes – which in most finals would easily have been the best goal of the game – and a Kevin Reeves penalty early in the second half, after Miller had pushed Bennett over in the box on fifty minutes had taken them into a slender lead. But a Man City victory would have been unjust. Spurs might not have been playing their best football of the season but Glenn Hoddle and Ossie Ardiles were (as ever) in splendid form in the heart of midfield, and whereas in the first match they'd shown craft but little graft, in the replay they showed both in equal measure. Hoddle created the Spurs equalizer on seventy minutes. A pinpoint pass beat the City defence and found the feet of Archibald, whose stabbed cross-shot fell to the feet of Crooks to score. The scene was set for Villa's show-stealing finale, easily the best goal of the match, perhaps the best in Wembley Cup final history. City tried to force a second equalizer, and very nearly succeeded when hole-in-his-heart substitute Dennis Tueart hit the very last shot of the game just wide of Spurs goalie Aleksic's post.

Long after Steve Perryman trudged up the thirty-nine steps and received the famous silver pot from the Queen (and the traditional bobble hat and scarf from the fans) the fans carried on chanting, to honour their bearded South American hero, 'Argentina, Argentina'.

I was there ... Garth Crooks

The thing that I always remember about the build-up to playing in the FA Cup final was Ossie Ardiles. He was such an example to me and I think to many of the players. He was the focal point of the team. In the League games between the semi-final and the final I found it hard to play as normal, I was worried about getting injured, my mind was elsewhere, but Ossie was as committed as ever. I mean this guy had played in a World Cup final, he'd done it all, yet here he was at places like the Goldstone Ground in Brighton inspiring the team. I found it amazing that he and Ricky Villa, who'd won the World Cup with Argentina, saw playing in the FA Cup final at Wembley as a real highlight of their career. That was their perception of this competition, which they'd only ever seen from afar, and they felt immensely proud to be in the midst of all this pomp and ceremony.

The final, of course, is more remembered for Ricky Villa and the great irony of his substitution and then his scoring the winning goal in the replay. On the Friday before the first match I remember Barry Davies interviewing the team for the BBC in our hotel, and they got Ricky's family on a satellite link. Then the following day he was unceremoniously hauled off, with the whole of Argentina watching, and I'll never forget watching the video of the match later and seeing him trudge all the way round the Wembley pitch. Ricky was a quiet, dignified man, so no one really knew how he felt about it afterwards. But in the days between the matches I felt that the same team should be given another crack – it's a cliché but we knew we hadn't won the battle, and that's why we hadn't won the war – and I was very happy for Ricky when Keith Burkinshaw said he was going to name the same team. I think that in a Cup final it's very easy for the moment to overtake you, nerves can rob you of your performance. I don't know this of course, but I think maybe Ricky's performance in the first final is an indication of how in awe he was of the whole event.

In the second match it was as if we had the real Ricky Villa back. He started like a whirlwind, scoring our first goal. But again we struggled a bit, and halfway through the second half we were 2–1 down and the game was beginning to drift away from us. We were a bit ragged, and it took a bit of vision from Glenn Hoddle to create a chance for us. I don't remember much about my goal, it was hardly a classic; all I do know is that the feeling was more one of relief than jubilation when it went in.

Ricky's goal, of course, was different. I'll never forget it. Ricky had a tendency to cut in from the by-line, which is exactly what he did on this occasion, and I was facing him on the edge of the box. He kept coming towards me, he just kept coming, and I couldn't get out of the way. So I had to just put my arms up to let him know he'd have to go past me as well as half the Man City defence, which he did. Then I turned round and saw him calmly go past Nicky Reid, round the keeper and put it in. It was typical Ricky, he had such composure, he was so calm on the ball.

When the final whistle went it was like this release, it was like re-living everything that had led up to winning the Cup, things like being an apprentice and scoring in the third round. And for me, it was my first real achievement in football. I've got a video of the match at home but I've only watched it once I think. I've got my own memories.

20

Manchester United 4   Benfica 1
(full-time score 1–1)
European Cup final
Wembley Stadium, attendance 100,000
29 May 1968

Ten years on from the Munich air disaster, and a year after Celtic had become the first British club to win the European Cup, a packed Wembley crowd expected glory for Matt Busby and his talented team. But despite the emphatic scoreline, this victory didn't come easily for a blue-clad United. On a night full of heroes, perhaps the greatest was United keeper Alex Stepney, who pulled off a magnificent save from Eusebio in the dying minutes of normal time, with the score at 1–1 and the Portuguese rampant. Eusebio's sporting acknowledgement of Stepney's save, and Stepney's no-nonsense don't-patronize-me-mate thump up the pitch said a great deal for United's superior determination that night.

The match started cautiously, and with two Portuguese defenders nullifying George Best, and Nobby Stiles handcuffed to Eusebio, the only forward to show any flair in the first half was the unsung United winger John Aston. But in the second half United piled forward and took a deserved lead in the fifty-fourth minute when skipper Bobby Charlton met Sadler's cross with his famous pate to guide the ball accurately past the Portuguese keeper. But after that they lacked the killer touch, and on the break Jaime Graca equalized for Benfica on seventy-eight minutes, before piling into the massed ranks of photographers. Only determined defending and that Stepney save in the closing minutes stood between United and defeat.

Busby had a task and a half to rally his troops in the break, but, like Alf Ramsey on the same pitch two years before, he did the business. 'If you pass the ball to each other, you've got the beating of them. When you get into the box, steady yourselves,' he said. His words had the desired effect: extra-time saw the Blue Devils find an extra dimension. Three minutes into the first period Best picked up a flick from birthday-boy teenager Brian Kidd, negotiated his way through a couple of tackles on a mazy twenty-five-yard run, drew the keeper and coolly slotted home from the penalty spot. Kidd, playing instead of the injured Law, had the night of his life, heading in the third and setting up Charlton for the fourth, a swivelling shot on the turn that had the Wembley crowd, all Union Jacks and tears of emotion, in raptures.

Bobby Charlton, famously, cried that night before lifting the huge silver cup up to the roaring crowd, the first Englishman to do so. But the most touching scenes afterwards were of Matt Busby, suited and booted in black, running on to the pitch to celebrate with his team. The victory was a tribute to the victims of the Munich disaster, and to the skill and passion of the third great team he built.

I was there . . . Pat Crerand

It was fantastic, especially for Matt Busby, it was the one he wanted to win so much. Because Matt didn't want to tempt fate by booking a hotel before we'd qualified for the final, we couldn't get a London hotel so we had to stay out in Egham in Surrey. But that was great, we just trained and relaxed there for three days. No press were allowed. The mood was very light-hearted, we were certain that we would win. We'd played Benfica a couple of years before and won 5–1 so we were very confident.

On the way to Wembley it was incredible. There were United supporters everywhere, and even people who followed other teams were supporting us. We were representing England and the streets were lined with people. It was a very warm, clammy night, and the only thing Matt said to us before the match was to keep the ball and make sure we didn't have to chase around on the Wembley pitch. In the first ninety minutes we should have won about 4–0. We were always the better side and always confident that we were going to do it. They did have a spell of pressure after they equalized and Alex made his save. I think Eusebio should have taken it round him but I think he saw those big bulging Wembley nets and wanted the glory of smashing it in; fortunately he hit it straight at Alex.

After ninety minutes we were still confident and Matt just said, 'Keep the ball and the goals will come,' though I don't think he would have believed how quickly. And after we'd gone a couple into the lead we didn't feel tired at all, we wanted to carry on playing all night.

After we won it was just incredible. Lifting the Cup, the atmosphere and Matt's delight. At the hotel when we got back there was a banquet and, this shows just what a great club United is, all the relatives of those that had died at Munich had been invited. In that way it was a very sad night, to think that some of them might have been playing instead of some of us.

21

Liverpool 3   Manchester United 3
Carling Premiership
Anfield, attendance 42,795
4 January 1994

anchester United would probably have settled for a point at Liverpool in the Championship-winning season of 1993/4, but not twenty-five minutes into this match when, after a stunning early performance, they were three goals up.

United had been in superb form all season, losing only once, and in the top spot since late August. Liverpool had got over a desperate patch in August and, having scrabbled up to seventh place, could start to think about a place in Europe. The fixture, traditionally one of the biggest in the calendar, is always a close, hard-fought, often low-scoring affair. But funny things happen in football during the Christmas and New Year period (although at this game the United fans weren't laughing all that loud).

And it all seemed so easy. Early in the match Bruce Grobbelaar, nearing the end of his Liverpool career, threw a characteristic wobbly as his defence allowed Steve Bruce to steal in with a typically powerful header. Shortly afterwards, Ryan Giggs, who'd been in fine form all season, outpaced the Liverpool defence to slot in a second with a slide-rule shot. Then, in the twenty-third minute, United got a free kick outside the box and Denis Irwin smacked one of his long-range specials to put the (all-black) Red Devils into an unassailable lead. Well, a seemingly unassailable lead.

What happened next should be shown to every team to stop their heads going down when they're on the end of a drubbing. Within a minute, Nigel Clough pulled one back. The match picked up pace with both sides going hell for leather to score and creating chances at both ends. Surely a fourth United goal would have sewn matters up? But it was Liverpool who got the break, Clough slotting in a second before half-time, his last goal for the club and indeed his last in Premiership football until his Manchester City debut. Liverpool had the impetus and the roar of the Kop to urge them on to an equalizer. Centre-half Bruce may have started things off with a headed goal, his counterpart Neil 'Razor' Ruddock emulating the feat to round off events. At 3–3 both sides could have scored in the finale – if either side had, perhaps this game would have been much higher up this list.

United, of course, never lost their top spot in the division, and finished the season repeating their 1992/3 Championship triumph. The demoralizing effect of a 4–3 defeat after being three up might well have changed all that.

I was there . . . Martin Tyler

The thing about sitting up in a TV gantry in freezing cold wind and rain is that if you're commentating on a match like this you feel as warm as toast. It was just a glorious expression of the best football that the Premiership can produce. It was the speed and the spectacle, it was just an incredible match.

When United went three goals up I can remember the director cut to Graeme Souness and it looked like everyone on the bench around him was leaning away from him. I'm sure they weren't really but that's what it looked like. I don't usually remember my comments in matches, but I will never forget on this occasion saying: 'Graeme Souness, a solitary figure at the club where you're never supposed to walk alone.'

It all seemed so poignant at the time, but of course by the end of the match Liverpool had come away with a psychological victory, and in the end they could have won it. Nigel Clough was their unlikely hero because he was going through a rough time, but after his two goals anything could have happened. United could have won 5–2 or Liverpool could have won. Liverpool ended so strongly but in the first half an hour United were awesome, with Cantona and Giggs deadly on the breakaway.

It was a simply breathtaking spectacle and undoubtedly one of the best matches I've ever had the privilege to witness. A true classic.

22

Celtic 2   Leeds 1
European Cup Winners' Cup semi-final, second leg
Hampden Park, attendance 136,505
15 April 1970

If they'd let anyone else into Hampden Park on 15 April 1970 they'd have had to stand on the pitch. Such feverish interest in this game was hardly surprising for this match would determine not only who'd go through to the European Cup Winners' Cup final but who was crowned 'Champions of Britain'.

With 136,000 packed into the stadium, the biggest crowd ever to attend a European tie, it was clear that for the people of Glasgow there was much more at stake here than a trip to Milan. Celtic had already won the first leg at Elland Road 1–0 thanks to a goal from Connelly after forty-five seconds, but Leeds repaid the compliment in the return, taking the lead after fourteen minutes and stunning the fanatical crowd. Billy Bremner took a pass from Johnny Giles and fired an astonishing shot over the defence and past Williams in the Celtic goal from thirty yards, and the scores were level on aggregate.

It stayed that way until half-time with the crowd roaring Celtic forward to no avail. Two minutes into the second half, however, John Hughes got the equalizer to send the crowd into delirium, glancing a header past Leeds keeper Sprake from Auld's cross. Six minutes later Sprake was carried off, his knee injured in a collision with Hughes, and before substitute keeper Harvey could get his bearings he was picking Bobby Murdoch's thunderous shot out of the back of the net. Cue the celebrations. After the final whistle the delirious Celtic fans refused to leave, remaining in the ground for twenty minutes and demanding a lap of honour.

Maybe it was over-confidence, maybe winning this match had left them drained, but three weeks later, despite taking the lead in the San Siro, Celtic lost the final 2–1 in extra-time to a Feyenoord side they should have beaten comfortably. 'We had too many players off-form,' said Jock Stein. But even in defeat, the Leeds victory was still being celebrated in Glasgow. In fact, it still is.

I was there . . . Billy McNeill

Oh, the atmosphere was just incredible. Often you weren't aware of the crowd when you were playing, but on this night you couldn't get away from it. The noise was incredible. The thing about playing for Celtic was that you always got great support, but this was better than anything I'd ever experienced before, the match meant so much.

There's no doubt that it was an England v. Scotland thing, but also there was this feeling that whoever won this tie would go on and win the Cup. Leeds had such a good side at that time, and I remember hoping that we missed them when the draw for the semi-finals was made. Anyway, it was such a big game that we were really prepared, we were all really up for it. We'd gone to Leeds and got a good result, but we knew it wasn't over, it was only half-time. Then they scored. Billy Bremner hit an incredible shot from thirty yards. I remember it flying past my head and I thought, 'I hope that's not on target.' But we were an attacking side and, if we went behind, we always felt we had the ability and the appetite, as well as the power of thought, to get goals back. That's the way we played and it's how it turned out. John Hughes scored for us although I remember being more worried when it was 1–1 than when Leeds were winning, because I knew then that if they got another they were through on away goals.

Anyway, Bobby Murdoch got the winner with a cracking shot and we did it. The crowd went absolutely mad, it was mayhem. It was such a big, big game that in many ways it cheated us out of the final. We were too confident and too complacent in the final against Feyenoord, and we lost. Someone should have done his homework on the rise of Dutch football, I don't think we even had them watched. They were a good side, a really good side, but we should have beaten them.

23

France 3 Portugal 2
(full-time score 1–1)
European Championship semi-final
Vélodrome, Marseilles, attendance 55,000
23 June 1984

The greatest night for the greatest-ever French team. Platini, Giresse, Tigana et al may have lifted the trophy in the Parc des Princes after beating Spain 2–0 four days later, but this was the night when they proved they were the worthy champions of Europe.

In the electric atmosphere of the Vélodrome on a balmy summer night, the French were roared to a scintillating victory against a superbly skilful Portuguese team who came oh-so-close to breaking the hearts of a nation. After ninety minutes it was 1–1 – Jordão's seventy-third-minute strike had cancelled out Domargue's twenty-fourth-minute opener for the French – and the match would be decided in extra-time. Seven minutes into the first period, Portuguese striker Jordão netted his second goal of the game. The crowd was stunned, but only momentarily, and it might have been just about the best thing that could have happened to the French. For a team where even the goalkeeper looked at his best going forward, chasing the game was probably preferable to defending a lead. Now it was all or bust and the dream team French midfield moved into overdrive. The noise was deafening as they charged forward, the hopes and dreams of the entire country weighing on their shoulders.

The French pushed while the Portuguese defended heroically, but with just six minutes of extra-time remaining the shield was finally pierced when French left-back Domargue scored again to make it 2-2. The relief and the euphoria combined into one mighty roar, but it didn't stop there. With the passion erupting from the terraces and the Portuguese rocking, the great Tigana broke away, beat three defenders and squared it to Platini. And with less than a minute to go, the French captain hammered home his eighth and best goal of the tournament. The Vélodrome erupted and France went wild: 'les Bleus' were in the final.

The final against Spain was a tighter affair, but the right team won. Platini scored the first (his ninth out of France's fifteen in the tournament) and Bellone wrapped it up, finishing a last-minute breakaway. It would have been a travesty had this great team won nothing, yet this match against Portugal was the only one of three major tournament semi-finals in four years from which this great French team emerged victorious. It was very nearly three out of three.

24

Argentina 3   Holland 1
(full-time score 1–1)
World Cup final
River Plate Stadium, Buenos Aires, attendance 77,000
25 June 1978

A badly refereed, bad-tempered end to a badly refereed, bad-tempered tournament, but a cracker none the less.

This match will be remembered for the feeble Italian referee, Argentina's gamesmanship, Holland's fifty fouls, the ticker-tape-strewn pitch – and Mario Kempes. Kempes was the star of the show, the tournament's top scorer with six goals and the saving grace of an Argentinian side that had relied a good deal on refereeing decisions (and some say bribery) to proceed to the final in front of their manic fans. The left-footed Valencia striker, the only foreign-based player in the team, allied a devastating shot with a cool head, and the hip-swivelling ability to slalom his way through defences. Argentina also boasted the cunning talents of Osvaldo Ardiles in midfield, and in Daniel Passarella, the current national coach, they had a leader in defence. Holland still had eight members of their 1974 World Cup final team in place, including Neeskens, Rep, Haan, Rensenbrink and van der Kerkhof, but were without Johan Cruyff, who despite a great deal of pressure had decided not to take part in the tournament.

The match kicked off nearly ten minutes late after Argentina stayed in their dressing-room seven minutes too long, only to complain about the light plaster cast on van der Kerkhof's wrist (which he'd worn without any problems from the beginning of the tournament) when they did turn up. Dutch skipper Neeskens was furious, and was just about to lead his players off the pitch when the referee decided to let the plaster cast remain on the wrist. But the incident led to a huge amount of bad feeling that manifested itself in vicious and uncharacteristic Dutch tackles on Ardiles and Bertoni within five minutes.

The Dutch started the stronger team and might have scored twice in the first half but for two great saves by keeper Fillol, from Rep and Rensenbrink. Then Argentina started playing the ball about, and Kempes put the home side ahead on thirty-eight minutes with a left-foot belter of a shot after Ardiles and Mexican bandit impersonator Luque teed up a chance. The Dutch poured forward in the second half, and it was Argentina's turn to put the boot in. But they couldn't stop substitute Nanninga's equalizer eight minutes from time, a header from van der Kerkhof's cross. And they weren't finished yet. Fillol in the Argentinian goal was beaten in the last minute by a belting shot from Rensenbrink. The massive crowd held its breath . . . the ball hit the post.

Before extra-time chain-smoking Cesar Luis Menotti galvanized his seemingly spent men. Kempes skipped round three men and a ton of ticker tape on his way to his second goal. And with the tired Dutch streaming forward, the man of the tournament finished things off by setting up Bertoni with a neat one-two for a third to spark the mother of all parties in Buenos Aires.

25

Brazil 5   Sweden 2
World Cup final
Rasunda Stadium, Stockholm, attendance 49,737
29 June 1958

This was the tournament that alerted the world to the talents of a certain teenage prodigy from Brazil: Edson Arantes do Nascimento, better known simply as Pelé. In Sweden the seventeen-year-old who was to become the world's greatest-ever player inspired a joyous team to a joyous victory over the home nation.

Brazil were managed by Vicente Feola, whose 4–2–4 formation was geared to attack from first minute to last. They boasted the talents of Didi in midfield, the thirty-year-old Vava in attack and Manoel Garrincha on the right wing. The 'little bird' was one of the best wing-forwards in the history of the game despite having a disfigured leg as the result of a bout of polio in his childhood, although he only made it into the team on the insistence of his team-mates. Manager Feola feared he was too inconsistent. On their day the South Americans were unstoppable, and they shifted into top gear in the semi-final with a 5–2 drubbing of France.

Sweden, on the other hand, were boosted by their talented 'Italian Brigade'. This group of players included centre-forward Gunnar Nordhal, inside-right 'Professor'

Gunnar Gren, and inside-left Nils Liedholm, all of whom played for Milan in a famous triumvirate nicknamed by the imaginative Italians the Gre-No-Li. They also had the advantage of the support of a hugely vociferous and patriotic home crowd. Sweden's English manager George Raynor had predicted that an early Sweden goal would see the South Americans crumble. He was forced to eat his words. Liedholm scored after four minutes . . . but the Brazilians hardly seemed to notice.

Within six minutes Vava had scored from a Garrincha cross after the winger had left the Swedish defence for dead, and they took the lead with an almost identical effort. The best moment of the game came, predictably, from Pelé, ten minutes into the second half. Tightly marked in the box, the young inside-left trapped the ball on his thigh, flicked it over his head, turned and volleyed it into the net to put Brazil 3–1 up, a goal that still rates among the best in World Cup final history. Goals from Zagalo and (an offside) Simonssen made the score 4–2, and the stage was set for Pelé to get his second in the game, and sixth in a tournament he didn't start, with an athletic header from a Zagalo cross. A star was born, and he promptly burst into tears of joy. And Brazil proved that, contrary to popular opinion, South American teams could travel, and travel in some style.

26

Italy 3   West Germany 1
World Cup final
Bernabeu, Madrid, attendance 90,000
11 July 1982

This was a final contested by two teams that had begun the tournament in shocking form. Italy had drawn their three group one matches, scraping a 1–1 draw with Cameroon to qualify by virtue of scoring one more goal than the Africans. They suddenly flowered in the second phase of the competition with the emergence of goalscoring sensation Paolo Rossi. Thanks to their new-found attacking flair they disposed of Argentina and, famously, Brazil in their group match and then Poland in the semi.

West Germany lost their opening encounter against Algeria in one of the shocks of the tournament, and played out a sterile 1–0 win over Austria in the final match of the opening group, a result which sickened any neutrals unfortunate enough to witness the game. The result suited both teams, and after an early goal the Teutonic neighbours just passed the ball to one another. West Germany made themselves more unpopular with the Spanish fans by knocking France out in the semis with the help of a brutal foul by goalkeeper Schumacher

on Battiston, which had left the Frenchman bereft of
two teeth and had, remarkably, gone unpunished.

The crowd were baying for Italy, if only as the lesser
of two evils. But the noise level dropped during a sterile
opening phase. The tactics were negative, both teams
more interested in stopping the opposition from playing
rather than setting the pace themselves. There was only
one moment of excitement in the first forty-five minutes,
when Italy were awarded a twenty-fourth-minute
penalty, Breitner lunging in on little Bruno Conti after
Altobelli's pass found him free in the box. With normal
spot-kick king Antonioni in the stands, Cabrini stepped
up to take it and, for the first time in a World Cup final,
missed, sidefooting the ball past the post.

In the second half Italy stepped up a gear. Tardelli
took a free kick (the umpteenth of the game) and spotted
Gentile free on the right. Gentile, for once in creative
mode after spending the game attached to Littbarski's
shirt, crossed to leave the German defence flat-footed.
Rossi, typically, reacted first, running into space to score
his sixth of the tournament. The game had needed a
goal like a junkie needs a fix, and the Germans, at last,
were dragged kicking and screaming out of their shells.
But they still found it hard to create anything to trouble
the competent Italian defenders. Eventually manager
Jupp Derwall brought on Hors Hrubesch, who vexed
Dino Zoff more than Fischer had done, making the
forty-year-old keeper scramble to save a header on his
line.

But gaps were opening for Italy, and their superb
sweeper Scirea (late and much lamented) burst from

defence, swapped passes with Rossi and freed Marco Tardelli on the edge of the box. Tardelli, man of the match, moved across the penalty area before falling over and scoring in one movement, thrashing the ball passed a bemused Schumacher, who was a sight for sore eyes. As was Tardelli, who went on to perform the best goal celebration of the tournament, sprinting away from his team-mates, both fists clenched, open-mouthed and eyes popping out in triumph, showing the world what a wonderful feeling it is to score a match-winner in a World Cup final. The Italian celebrations weren't over, though. Young substitute Altobelli, who had been playing from as early as the seventh minute after veteran Graziani picked up an injury, finished the Germans off, coolly stopping Conti's pass before placing the ball beyond Schumacher. Paul Breitner hit a consolation goal past Zoff, but it was too little, too late for the Germans.

Italian manager Enzo Bearzot, a hated figure just two weeks previously, was suddenly a national hero. It would be an audacious claim to say the wily Italian told his players to save themselves in the opening matches in order to turn it on for the big occasion, but Bearzot did motivate his team when it really mattered, and managed to beat the back-stabbing Italian press as well as the best opponents the world could offer.

27

England 1   West Germany 1
(a.e.t., 3–4 on penalties)
World Cup semi-final
Stadio delle Alpi, Turin, attendance 62,000
4 July 1990

Never in the field of football conflict has so much hope been given to so many by so few. England were agonizingly close to a place in the final, and Gascoigne wasn't the only one to cry that night.

England started as underdogs, but emerged from the tunnel raring to go and immediately won three corners on the trot. Gascoigne was at his sparkling best, dominating the midfield for long periods and often making Lothar Mattheus look average, at one point nutmegging the German captain. The rest of the team, too, were in fine form, working well as a cohesive unit, creating chances, looking every bit as good as the Germans. Even Terry Butcher managed to show some style with a little backheel in the first half. Then the Germans started to play, and it was England's turn to step on to the back foot. Shilton kept England in it, saving from Thon then fingertipping away a blistering Augenthaler free kick. Half-time, and no goals, but honours definitely shared.

Early in the second half a German goal looked

inevitable, and on fifty-nine minutes it arrived. Parker tried to charge down a Brehme free kick, the ball deflected off his leg, ballooned over a manically backpedalling Shilton and crept agonizingly under the bar. 1–0 to West Germany. David Platt ran into the goal to collect the ball, signalling a new sense of urgency for the English team. A Gascoigne free kick went wide. Illgner saved from Wright. England were pulling the Germans to full stretch. A German win in ninety minutes would have been an injustice and Lineker (who else?) redressed the balance with a fine goal ten minutes from time. As the ball fell to him just inside the box he beat Kohler and Augenthaler with his first touch, and skidded the ball between Illgner and his left-hand post with the second. Jubilation.

Extra-time yielded more chances, but no further goals. Waddle's long shot hit the post then Buchwald did the same for West Germany and the spectre of penalties loomed, then became reality. Poor Pearce, who blasted straight at Illgner. Poor Waddle, whose effort ended up somewhere in France. West Germany went on to win the tournament and England had to console themselves with the tag of gallant losers and the Fair Play Award, and the knowledge that, with West Germany lifting the trophy a few days later after a dreadful match with Maradona's Argentina, they'd played in the real final . . . and lost by a whisker.

I never even dreamed of the final or lifting the World Cup, but we knew that Italy were out and that if we did beat Germany then it was there for the taking.

The days before the game we spent at Juventus's training hideaway which was great, although we didn't do much training because so many players were carrying injuries. We'd just scraped through against Cameroon in extra-time thanks to Gary's cool head and it had taken a lot out of us, but the team spirit had really built up, like a real 'bad boys on tour' kind of thing. We knew the Germans would be the hardest team we were going to face but we fancied our chances. It was a great honour for me to be leading out the team on such an occasion and the team certainly didn't need much motivation. When I came out of the tunnel I always used to eyeball the opposition, and from the German faces I could see that they were afraid of us. It was always going to be a battle of nerves.

The match itself is all a blur really, I was so focused on the game and doing well that I can't really remember it. I've never watched it on video, either, I just couldn't bear it. I know that we started well but then they scored in the second half and we were up against it. The ball hit Paul Parker and it just seemed to hang in the air for ages before dropping over Shilts and I thought, 'Oh no, here we go again, just like Argentina in 1986 and the Hand of God.' I just thought, 'We've got to keep going.'

It was all over for me, though, when I was taken off in the sixty-fifth minute and we went back to four at the back, so I had to sit through the rest on the bench. When Gary scored we were all jumping around like nutters and I thought we were going to do it, and even in extra-time I thought we would sneak it, but it all became very tight and tense. When it came to penalties I just sat with Bobby Robson on the bench with our arms crossed. We were totally helpless. When Pearce and Waddle missed it was hard to take it all in, it didn't seem real.

Afterwards there was a lot of singing on the coach. The boys who'd missed the penalties were distraught but we knew that we had done ourselves, and the country, proud. It was only when I got back to the hotel, in the peace of my room, that I realized, 'My God, we were so close.'

28

Brazilian style, Brazilian pace and Brazilian goals. The Goodison Park crowd got what it came to see, but from the Hungarians and not the World Cup favourites. With Pelé out injured, hacked to submission by the Bulgarian defenders in Brazil's previous match, the stage was set for Hungary to display their own brand of skilful, stylish football and inflict Brazil's first defeat in a World Cup game since 1954.

It was a scintillating match played at awesome pace, full of skill, and punctuated by some exquisite goals. By the end of the match the crowd had a new hero and broke out into chanting the name of Albert, the Hungarian midfielder who orchestrated the downfall of Brazil with his passing, vision and superb dribbling. Albert was at the centre of everything the Hungarians created, always making the right choice, when to pass, when to beat a man, when to check back.

After just three minutes it was clear that the Brazilians, who never really came to terms with the European conditions and had Santos and Garrincha carrying injuries, were in trouble. Hungarian forward Bene danced his way in from the right and squeezed his shot past Gilmar from the narrowest of angles to make it 1–0. It was all Hungary from then on with attack after sweeping attack surging towards the Brazilian goal. When Brazil did threaten it seemed that the excellent Hungarian defence, with the grey-haired Matrai sweeping up behind the rock-solid pairing of Sipos and Meszoly, had everything under control. Hungary pressed but, thanks to a goal from the young Tostão – playing instead of Pelé – Brazil went in level at half-time, totally against the run of play.

In the second half the Hungarians were in full flow again, and this time they made relentless pressure count and their second goal epitomized the performance. Albert's clever run and pass found Bene tearing down the right again. Bene's fast low cross was met on the volley by Farkas and the ball smashed into the net. A Meszoly penalty right at the end made it 3–1 and capped one of the most thrilling performances the World Cup has ever seen. It was to prove the end for Brazil, but a new beginning for Hungary after the 1956 revolution had brought a premature end to the great Puskas era.

29

AC Milan 4   Steaua Bucharest 0
European Cup final
Nou Camp, Barcelona, attendance 100,000
24 May 1989

his wasn't a great contest, it was hardly a contest at all, but it must go down as one of the greatest team performances of all time. It's not that Steaua were a bad side, far from it. The Romanian army team included the likes of Hagi and Lacatus and had won the competition three years earlier against Terry Venables's Barcelona. But on the night, with wonderful performances from the Dutch trio of Rijkaard, Gullit and Van Basten, Milan were unstoppable.

This Milan side, built with the multi-millions of Italian business magnate and future prime minister Silvio Berlusconi and astutely managed by Arrigo Sacchi, had destroyed the virtual monopoly Juventus had enjoyed in Italy for over a decade, and eclipsed the Maradona-inspired Napoli revival. Sacchi provided the tactics to make Berlusconi's investment pay off, introducing an English-style up front 'pressing' that didn't allow the opposition any time on the ball, keeping tight at the back, and using short passing to devastate in attack. There wasn't really a weak link in the side, with Franco Baresi marshalling a young defence including twenty-one-year-old full-back sensation Paolo Maldini, a midfield that included internationals Ancelotti and Donadoni and then, of course, the Dutchmen. They had pummelled Real Madrid 5–0 in the San Siro leg of the semi-final, hitting form at the right time after scraping through the second and third rounds.

On a balmy Barcelona night they gelled to perfection. Gullit, only 60 per cent fit after a cartilage operation, won everything in the air, scored two magnificent goals and hit a post. Van Basten, not to be outdone, scored the other two, the second, set up by Rijkaard, his tenth in the competition. All this after forty-six minutes, and it looked as though Milan could score at will. Unfortunately Gullit was substituted after fifty-nine minutes, otherwise Milan might have broken the scoring record set by Real Madrid in the 1960 final. But as it was, the *Rossoneri* produced the best hour of attacking football this fixture had seen for two decades.

30

Congo 3 Mali 2
African Nations Cup final
Omnisports Stadium, Yaounde, Cameroon
5 March 1972

Widely regarded as the greatest African Nations Cup final ever, this was a humdinger of a match in the period that Emmanuel Maradas, editor of *African Soccer* magazine, describes as the 'golden era of African football'. The Red Devils of Congo and the Eagles of Mali provided a feast of attacking football in the days when there were few African professionals and even fewer defensive-minded coaches. 'This was just about the best African match ever,' enthuses Maradas. 'It was played in a fine sporting spirit by two fantastic sides whose only real thought was to attack. In those days no one copied the Europeans. If teams tried to copy anyone it was Brazil and the intention was always to go out and score more goals than the other team, not concede less.'

Amazingly the score stayed at 0–0 until the forty-second minute, with the Congo keeper Matsima performing heroics to keep Mali out. But he couldn't stop them taking the lead just before half-time. Two goals in seven minutes from M'Bono put Congo in front in the second half but with seventeen minutes remaining Mali star Bakaray Traore brought the scores level again. The pace was relentless as both sides charged forward in search of the winner but, with extra-time looming, it was Congo's M'Pelé who stole the glory with a goal in the dying seconds.

There's no doubt that African soccer has come a long way since this great match, and Pelé's assertion about an African World Cup victory before the turn of the century is quoted in every article you read about Tony Yeboah, George Weah or Finidi George. It's a pity there aren't a few videos of this game knocking about, however, to show those who dismissed African football out of hand for so many years.

31

Germany 3   England 6
Friendly
Olympic Stadium, Berlin, attendance 110,000
14 May 1938

It was supposed to be a show of Third Reich superiority
but turned out to be one of the greatest England
performances of all time. Sadly the match is better
remembered by many for the Nazi salute the English
players were ordered to give as they lined up before the
kick-off rather than the unforgettable display of football
in a match Sir Stanley Matthews recalls as his 'greatest
ever' for England. When the England players were told
they would have to make the salute Eddie Hapgood,
the England captain, insisted that standing to attention
would be sufficient. But the British ambassador Sir
Neville Henderson, afraid that refusal would be seen as
a snub to Goering and Goebbels in the crowd, ordered
the players to comply and was supported by FA Secretary
Stanley Rous.

With immense national pride at stake, the German
side that faced England had been specially selected after
months of trials and were fresh from ten days at a special
training centre. England, meanwhile, had made the long,
tiring journey to Germany over land and sea. But it made
no difference. With Matthews playing out of his skin and

running the German defence ragged, England stunned the 110,000 Berlin crowd with a masterful display. By half-time it was 2–4 and no doubt the Third Reich generals were relieved that Hitler hadn't been able to make it. The performance was sealed by a wonder goal from West Ham's Len Goulden. It started, inevitably, with Matthews, who'd already scored himself. Running at the defence yet again he outwitted the German full-back and fired another ball across the edge of the box. Goulden met the volley full on and the ball screamed into the net from twenty-five yards.

'It was by far and away the best England performance that I was ever involved in,' says Sir Stanley Matthews. 'No one gave us a hope. And for Len Goulden to score a goal like that with an old leather ball like we used then was incredible.' Don Welsh, who made his England debut in the match, said afterwards: 'You couldn't have asked for a better performance than this. Only when the heat got to us in the second half did we have to slow down. I honestly thought we could have scored ten.'

The match took place just after Germany had annexed Austria and the Germans had said that they would include Austrian players in their team for the match which was to mark the start of England's end-of-season European tour. However, they had agreed not to name any Austrians in their starting line-up in exchange for Aston Villa playing a friendly match against a combined German and Austrian team the following day. The Aston Villa players refused to give the Nazi salute and were jeered throughout the entire match.

I was there . . . Sir Stanley Matthews

Germany were the favourites because they had a great team at the time and they'd been in this special training camp in the Black Forest. We'd travelled by boat and train, which took about a day, but that didn't bother us. We were used to those sorts of journeys.

The stadium was absolutely magnificent, it was packed to the rafters, there must have been 100,000 people there but the atmosphere wasn't particularly hostile. We were put in a dressing-room right at the top of the stand. You had to go down about eighty steps, through a tunnel and then you came straight out on to the pitch. This meant that at half-time we had to climb back up all these steps to get to the dressing-room, but we were winning so we didn't mind.

Before the match there was all this talk about, 'Should we do the Nazi salute?' In the end the ambassador said that he thought we should. We just went along with it because we wanted to get on with the football, that's all we were thinking about; as far as we were concerned politics didn't come into it. This was a football match.

And it was a great match. We played very well and I scored, which was pretty unusual. The goal that Len Goulden scored, however, was probably the best goal I ever saw. If it was televised like the matches are these days, and shown in slow motion, there's plenty of people would say it's the best goal they've ever seen too.

32

West Germany 2   Holland 1
World Cup final
Olympic Stadium, Munich, attendance 77,833
7 July 1974

On the one hand we had West Germany, the hosts. A talented bunch, with Beckenbauer ruling defence alongside the assured Berti Vogts, and no fools in attack either with Gerd Muller, international goal-a-game scorer. On the other we had Holland, the neutrals' favourites, exponents of total football where defenders could attack, attackers defend and midfielders do what the hell they liked. Cruyff, of course, was the master: a gawky trickster who had taken on Pélé's mantle of world number one.

Holland made the most spectacular start in any World Cup final. Kicking off, they held possession for a full minute, stringing together fifteen passes across the defence and into midfield. Cruyff picked up the ball, and with a burst of pace and a flash of brilliance left his marker Vogts, no slouch, for dead and carried the ball into the box. Hoeness tried to make a saving tackle, but caught Cruyff's leg instead of the ball. Penalty. Neeskens blasted a right-footer, Maier was wrong-footed, 1–0. Early goals can be false friends, and this game seems to be a case in point. Holland dominated possession for the next twenty-five minutes, but lacked the killer instinct, weaving delicate spiders' webs without threatening goals.

Then German winger Holzenbein picked up a ball from Overath, surged into the box, and was himself upended by Jansen. Another penalty, another goal, this time for Breitner. West Germany were galvanized by the goal, setting up several chances, though leaving gaps at the back. The Germans came close to a second: first through Vogts who, leaving Cruyff for once, slammed a shot that Jongbloed tipped round; then from Hoeness, whose effort was kicked off the line; and then through Beckenbauer, whose delicate chip was fingertipped over the bar. Holland, for their part, could have snatched a lead when Cruyff cut out Beckenbauer and slipped the ball to Rep, one on one with Maier. The shot was saved.

Then on forty-three minutes Bonhof found mop-haired Muller in the box, who controlled with one foot and scored with his other, leaving Dutch defenders strewn around his feet. It was a brilliant goal, the sixty-second of his international career and by far the most valuable to his country. Try as they might Holland couldn't equalize, although Neeskens's volley from substitute van der Kerkhof's looping cross could have drawn things level had Sepp Maier not stretched to keep it out somehow. In fact West Germany were the more likely second-half scorers, with Muller's onside goal ruled offside and a second Jansen-on-Holzenbein penalty turned down by Welsh referee Clive Thomas. The people's favourites had lost, but gallantly, and the Germans had proved that their brand of total football was the stronger on the night.

33

Hungary 4   Uruguay 2
(full-time score 2–2)
World Cup semi-final
La Pontaise Stadium, Lausanne, Switzerland,
attendance 37,000
30 June 1954

This was the great Hungary side, the one that had
humiliated England 6–3 at Wembley and 7–1 in
Budapest, with the likes of Czibor, Hidegkuti and
Kocsis in its ranks, while the great Puskas, injured,
watched from the sidelines. Uruguay were also fresh
from a spot of England humiliation, having beaten
Matthews, Lofthouse, Finney et al 4–2 in the quarter-
final four days before.

Hungary's quarter-final against Brazil, meanwhile,
nicknamed the Battle of Berne, had been a real scrap.
And by that I mean a *real* scrap, with bottles flying in a
post-match dressing-room brawl which makes Ancona v.
Birmingham look like a game of Subbuteo. The heavens
opened before this semi-final, and never shut again, but
the two sides made light work of the heavy weather and
produced a truly classic match. The Hungarians, having
been threatened with retribution from Budapest if they
lost, played the match of their lives.

Uruguay, twice winners, had never been beaten in a
World Cup match, but Hungary started favourites. And

after fifteen minutes they took the lead with a volley
from the left-winger Czibor, and got another just after
half-time through Hidegkuti's headed goal. Losing 2–0,
Uruguay could have been down and out, but they rallied,
with Juan Schiaffino in superb form. Schiaffino set up
Hohberg (a naturalized Argentinian) to score with
fifteen minutes to go and three minutes from time the
duo put on a repeat performance to make it 2–2.
Hohberg was congratulated by his team-mates so vigorously he was knocked out cold. In extra-time the pair
combined yet again, but Uruguay hit the post, a signal
for Hungary to up the tempo. With the South Americans
down to ten men through injury, Kocsis headed two
memorable goals to take Hungary into the final.

'We beat the best team we have ever met,' said the
Hungarian manager Gyula Mandi after the match. He
had a right to be chuffed: it was an exhilarating game
despite the atrocious weather. And everything looked on
for a Hungarian victory celebration in the final as they
faced underdogs West Germany, a side they had slaughtered 8–3 in the qualifying round. A rout looked on the
cards after the Hungarians went two up in the first ten
minutes but, unbalanced by an injured Puskas who'd
insisted on playing and tired after their extra-time exertions against Uruguay, they lost 3–2 and go down in
history as the best team never to lift the World Cup. But
they showed the world their capabilities in the semi,
billed by many afterwards as the best game ever. England
captain Billy Wright said it was 'as near to perfection as
we will ever see'.

34

Manchester United 3   West Bromwich Albion 5
League Division One
Old Trafford, attendance 45,091
30 December 1978

This was surely the best West Bromwich Albion team of the last three decades, one that had fought for England in the Uefa Cup and was to qualify again at the end of the season. It was the classic Ron Atkinson team featuring the likes of Cyrille Regis, Tony and Ally Brown, Derek Statham, Tony Godden and a certain Bryan Robson. A fine side indeed, but nobody expected them to go and score five goals at Old Trafford.

West Brom were the form team, going into the game on the back of a ten-match unbeaten run. United, on the other hand, although they included in their ranks internationals such as Brian Greenhoff, Sammy McIlroy, Gordon McQueen, Steve Coppell, Martin Buchan, Stewart Houston and Mickey Thomas, had lost three of their last six matches, two of them by embarrassing 3–0 scorelines. Nevertheless Greenhoff appeared to set them on their way with a twenty-yard screamer from a left-wing corner. But Tony Brown equalized and then Len Cantello put the Baggies ahead with a magical goal which was voted Goal of the Season: Regis back-heeled superbly to find the number ten in space and Cantello hit the ball past Bailey's legs.

The game was a humdinger and it was United's turn to dominate. McQueen headed an equalizer, and McIlroy dribbled in United's third. Tony Brown equalized from short range and then, to give everybody a breather and let the crowd work out exactly what the score was, the half-time whistle blew. The only thing that let up in the second half was the number of goals – West Brom had to wait until the seventy-fifth minute for their fourth, Laurie Cunningham showing his speed to outsprint the United defence. Then Regis rounded things off with a deserved goal, an absolute thumper from an Ally Brown pass to put the game beyond United.

Ron Atkinson believes this to be 'the greatest game of all time'. I wonder why?

35

England 9 Scotland 3
Home International
Wembley Stadium, attendance 97,350
15 April 1961

'**W**hat's the time at Wembley? Nearly ten past
Haffey.' The joke was on Scottish keeper
Frank Haffey for days after England annihilated
the auld enemy at Wembley in 1961. OK, so Haffey's
performance wasn't exactly breathtaking that day, but
the England attack was.

Spearheaded by Jimmy Greaves, whose £80,000
transfer to AC Milan had just been signed and sealed,
and inspired by the cultured passing and deadly finishing
of Fulham's Johnny Haynes, Walter Winterbottom's
team ran riot. In fact, adopting long-ball tactics as
opposed to Scotland's intricate passing game, England
scored most of their goals on the counter-attack. Poor
Frank Haffey. He'd been called into the fray only because
of injuries to Scotland's first-choice keepers, but by the
time he trudged off the pitch he'd become a national
joke and Scotland's goalkeepers would never be treated
the same again. The story goes that not only did he let
in nine, Haffey further outraged his distraught team-
mates when they caught him whistling merrily in the
Wembley bath.

Showing the hapless keeper no mercy, Greaves scored a hat-trick, Johnny Haynes tore the defence to shreds with his pinpoint passing and scored twice himself, Bobby Smith got two and Bobby Robson and Bryan Douglas got one each. Against a sweeper system or a massed defence, this strikeforce might not have got much joy. But against a square defence and a team chasing the game, scoring goals was like taking milk from a baby. In fact, during the 1960/1 Home Championship England went on to score nineteen goals, equalling the record, as did Jimmy Greaves who scored seven in total. In fact, to this day Greaves's hat-trick in this match is the last to be scored in an England v. Scotland match.

Under Winterbottom England had won their last five games, scoring thirty-two goals with Greaves getting eleven of them. Greaves was on fire and on the way to Milan, the 'lure of the lire' persuading him to part from Stamford Bridge. Six months later he was back, bought by Tottenham for £99,999 because Bill Nicholson didn't want him to be saddled with the tag of 'the first £100,000 player'. Greaves eventually played for England fifty-seven times; Haffey never played for Scotland again.

I was there . . . Jimmy Armfield

Everyone goes on about Frank Haffey having a night-mare, but that's very unfair. He did make a couple of errors but so did a few of the Scottish players that day and it's all too easy to blame the keeper.

This was one of the best England teams I think we've ever had. We were a great side going forward. Walter

Winterbottom had been trying to keep a settled side and we'd had some great results coming up to this match and scored a lot of goals. It was a forceful team with a good touch. Jimmy Greaves of course was a great finisher, as good as we've ever had. Then there was Bobby Charlton who was always a penetrating player, Bryan Douglas who was very tricky and Robson and Haynes who were great passers of the ball.

It's hard to appreciate today what it was like playing Scotland. The noise made by the Scottish fans was incredible, many of them would save all year for the pilgrimage to Wembley. But we played a fast, attacking game with great mobility and some great finishing and it soon silenced the Scots in the crowd. It was a one-off result but at the time it was really special, especially against the old enemy. In Scotland they try to erase the game from the memory; if you tried to talk about it they'd change the subject.

If this England team had stayed intact then I think we could have won the World Cup in Chile the following year. But we lost Smith and Swan through injury and that took the heart out of the team, without them we didn't have the experience. We went to Chile and got beaten by Brazil in the quarter-finals, but if we'd played them six months earlier we might just have beaten them.

36

Coventry 3   Tottenham 2
(full-time score 2–2)
FA Cup final
Wembley Stadium, attendance 98,000
16 May 1987

This match had it all: own goals, a spectacular diving header, extra-time, and an underdog winner. Coventry lifted the Cup in the club's first-ever FA Cup final appearance.

No one had given them much of a chance. Coventry had struggled in the top flight that season, despite the charismatic managing duo of John Sillett and George Curtis, and had been flattered by a mid-table finish. But their Cup form had been inspired and they had put out Manchester United and Leeds on the way to Wembley. With Waddle, Hoddle, Ardiles and Clive Allen in the side, Tottenham were, however, an attacking force to be reckoned with, especially with David Pleat as their manager. Pleat had said before the game that he thought it had the makings of a classic, though he couldn't have predicted just how classic it would be and would have settled for a dull Spurs win if he'd known what was really going to happen.

The match started as the form book suggested, with an early goal for Spurs. Clive Allen put the north Londoners up after just two minutes, with his forty-ninth

137

goal of the season, a tap-in after a dazzling example of Waddle wizardry. A rout looked on the cards but Coventry were level within ten minutes, Bennett swivelling to score from close range after a cross from Greg Downs eluded both Clemence and Hodge. This was the cue for Waddle and Hoddle to turn on the style, and it was a bit of Glenda magic that led to Tottenham's deserved half-time lead, his flighted free kick deflected by a miserable Brian Kilcline into his own net. Coventry showed fighting spirit by coming back in the second half, and produced a stunning goal that still lives fresh in the memory. Bennett curled in a cross that fooled the Spurs defence, and Houchen, completely horizontal, scored a diving header the like of which Wembley will be lucky to see again.

After such a spectacular ninety minutes, either side would have been unfortunate to lose. But no one was as unfortunate as Gary Mabbutt when McGrath's cross bounced off him and skewed over Clemence and into his own net six minutes into extra-time. Try as they might, tired Spurs just couldn't make the breakthrough they needed to take the game to a replay. The lid-on-the-head celebrations were all Coventry's and only half of north London begrudged them their celebrations. There's no doubt that Tottenham were the more skilful side, but on the day they'd been outflanked by Coventry's superior cut-and-thrust strategy. And while it was skipper Brian 'Caveman' Kilcline who, teeth gritted into a smile, lifted the Cup up to the fans, the dancing management team Curtis and Sillett deserved most of the plaudits.

COVENTRY 3   TOTTENHAM 2

I was there . . . Keith Houchen

It's funny. You work your bollocks off in football, like I'm doing now at Hartlepool, for hardly any recognition, but you score in an FA Cup final and it follows you around for ever. Not that I'm complaining. Oh no, I think I've seen the goal from every angle, I've got pictures of it from every angle, in fact we've got a new lounge here at Hartlepool and I've made them put a big black and white picture of it up in there!

I always dreamed of playing in an FA Cup final. From around 1977 I stood on the terraces at Wembley for about five finals in a row, so to actually get out on the pitch on the biggest stage of the lot was incredible. All through the Cup run that year we just had this feeling that we were going to get to Wembley. There was such a good team spirit at Coventry at that time and we had some real characters at the club, people like Brian Kilcline and Trevor Peake. We had a good side as well, and during the Cup matches we seemed to play with no inhibitions at all. We had no fear. All our matches seemed to be good, attacking games, and it all culminated in getting to Wembley. And when we got there, we really set out to enjoy the day.

When they scored after two minutes, though, I think that was the first time we showed any apprehension. I think a few of the lads looked at each other and sort of said, 'Let's not take a hammering with millions of people watching.' But we always seemed to bounce back, and a few minutes later we were level.

At half-time we were 2–1 down but we weren't

worried. We were enjoying ourselves and it was an open, attacking game which suited us. We knew we'd get more chances. Then, of course, came the best goal of the game. I played the ball out to Dave Bennett and then set off to get into the box at breakneck speed for me, which is quite a lot behind anyone else. When the ball came across the only way I was going to get to it was by throwing myself at it, and they always look spectacular if they go in like that . . . although of course it was a very well-directed header!

It was only afterwards that it sank in that not only had we won the FA Cup, but that it had been a thrilling match, and it's nice that people think of it as one of the classics.

37

Real Madrid 0   Ajax 2
Uefa Champions League group D
Bernabeu Stadium, Madrid, attendance 82,500
22 November 1995

Ajax teams will always have to stand the test of comparison with the great Cruyff-inspired team which won three European Cups on the trot in the 1970s. But if the current side carries on playing like this, they could go on to achieve even more than their 'total football' predecessors.

Eighty thousand Spaniards turned up in the hope of seeing Real Madrid live up to their great history and topple the current European Cup holders. But by the end of the match the Spanish crowd was applauding a stunning display of team football that currently makes Ajax the undisputed kings of world football. In fact, for Real, 2–0 was a let-off. In an amazing early blitz Overmars, Litmanen and Kluivert all hit the crossbar and a goal that had clearly crossed the line was disallowed, as was another for a highly dubious offside decision. At the home of the most famous name in European football, Ajax ran riot. The way he played, Ghana's Finidi George seemed almost telepathically linked to the Dutchmen Kluivert and Overmars and the Finn Litmanen. 'It's as fine a performance as I've ever seen,' says Archie

McPherson who commentated on the match for Euro-sport. 'The thing about them is that there's no one outstanding star, it's just a truly outstanding team.'

In the second half the movement, passing and vision of the young team finally reaped its rewards, Litmanen and Kluivert scoring in a ten-minute burst of brilliance. After the match the massive Madrid crowd rose as one to acknowledge and applaud the new champions of Europe and Real coach Jorge Valdano said: 'Ajax are not just the team of the 1990s, they are approaching footballing Utopia.' A few weeks later Ajax were crowned World Club Champions after beating Gremio (albeit on penalties) and a few months after that they lifted the European Super Cup following a thumping victory over Real Zaragoza.

With their celebrated youth development system and a style of play that has the world purring in admiration (and Italian club owners reaching for their chequebooks), Ajax are the modern face of football. And when Kluivert, Davids and Overmars are gone, the chances are there will be three more young Dutchmen who know 'the Ajax way' inside out ready to slot neatly into the side.

38

Charlie George thunders the ball into the Liverpool net, flops on to his back with his arms aloft, and waits for the Arsenal players to engulf him. Arsenal has done the Double and the darling of the North Bank scored the winner. In a season when Leeds were expected to clean up yet won nothing, Arsenal had pipped them to the League and survived away draws in every round to lift the Cup at Wembley.

With so much at stake – Arsenal having clinched the League title at White Hart Lane a few days earlier – this was always going to be a tense match. With Liverpool conceding only twenty-four League goals all season and Arsenal's comparable strength at the back, it was no surprise that it was a tight affair. At the time of normal time it was 0–0 and although Arsenal had created enough to join the exclusive ranks of the Double winners' club, Shankly's Liverpool were still in it. Two minutes into extra-time they were in front thanks to Steve Heighway and Bob Wilson's lapse which allowed the Liverpool winger's shot to creep in at his near post. Suddenly the temperature was raised and Arsenal were soon level. John

Radford hooked the ball into the area and Eddie Kelly pushed a weak shot towards goal. Man of the match George Graham made a 'did he, didn't he touch it' lunge at the ball as it crossed the line. Arsenal didn't care who scored, as long as it was 1–1. Then, eight minutes from time, it was Charlie George's moment of glory. The flamboyant Highbury-born Gunner unleashed that famous scorcher from Radford's pass and guaranteed himself a regular appearance on the *Match of the Day* titles. He had graduated from being a lad who supported Arsenal from the North Bank, to the man who won them the Double at Wembley. Combining brilliant, powerful football with sheer professionalism and hard work Bertie Mee's side had triumphed and, at last, laid to rest the ghost of the great Arsenal sides of the past.

I was there . . . Frank McLintock

To be honest it was all a bit of an anti-climax for me. Don't get me wrong, I was jubilant, but I was so exhausted and so relieved that we hadn't thrown the Double away that I never felt the ecstasy that I expected. Bob Wilson said that they couldn't hold me back from 'running up the steps'. That's the biggest exaggeration I've ever heard. I crawled up those steps, literally. I had felt the joy the fans were feeling as we lifted the Cup on the Monday before when we'd beaten Tottenham to win the League at White Hart Lane. Now it was like I'd given everything and I had nothing left. I'd played in every game that season, pre-season matches, friendlies,

George Best celebrates with the European Cup. Which seems fair as Manchester United would never have won it without his domination in extra-time.

Above: **Brazil's** 1970 team is still reputed to be the best football team of all time. And the best game they played on their way to winning the Jules Rimet trophy was their 1-0 victory over England.

Opposite page: **Celtic's Lisbon Lions** were the first British team to win the European Cup and skipper Billy McNeill collected the trophy. He was used to collecting cups that season: he'd already picked up the League Championship, the Scottish Cup and the League Cup.

Michael Thomas' last-minute goal guaranteed that
the 1989 title race finished in the most dramatic fashion
possible. Arsenal had to win by two to leapfrog Liverpool;
Thomas' strike made sure that they did precisely that.

Italy weren't expected to win the 1982 World Cup. But then no one expected Paolo Rossi to finish as the tournament's top scorer; his six goals included the two in the semi, and the first of Italy's three against Germany in the final.

Paul Gascoigne was in tears during the Italia 1990 semi. A yellow card meant he'd miss the final. So in a nice show of solidarity the rest of the England team, led by Stuart Pearce and Chris Waddle, decided to give it a miss as well.

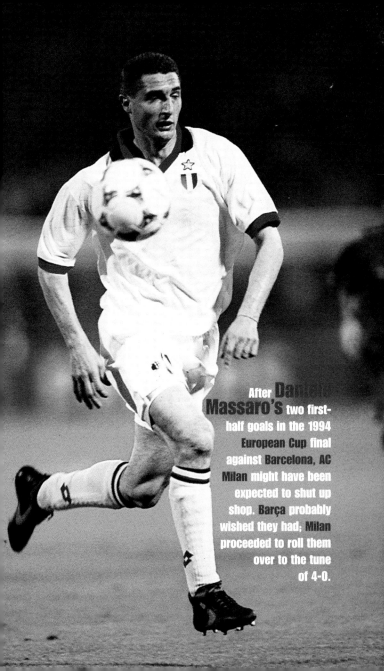

After Daniele Massaro's two first-half goals in the 1994 European Cup final against Barcelona, AC Milan might have been expected to shut up shop. Barça probably wished they had; Milan proceeded to roll them over to the tune of 4-0.

Stuart McCall drew first blood in his battle with **Steve McMahon** in the 1989 Merseyside Cup Final, on as sub he scored twice. But sadly for him his two were eclipsed by Ian Rush's winning double strike.

replays, testimonials, everything. And as captain you've got to organize, control, keep people on their toes and give others a pat on the back. So when it was all over, and we'd done it, it was like my battery had run flat. Afterwards I had to have a few drinks, almost to cheer myself up.

Before the match we were all very focused. The Double was on, although we didn't mention it, but the expectation was so great that it was only something we could throw away. We'd banned all talk of the Double in the dressing-room, and we'd banned all talk of being tired. We knew that the match against Liverpool would be very tough. It was ninety degrees on the Wembley pitch and they were supposed to be the fittest team in the League, so Bill Shankly always used to say anyway. I saw it recently though and it was a good match, with a lot of quality passing. It was a tight game as matches against Liverpool and Leeds always were: they were seldom high-scoring games because of the quality of the defenders. You had to do something special just to earn a shot at goal.

Then we went a goal down and we had to just stick in there, hoping we'd get lucky. Which we did, and then in extra-time Charlie George won us the match. He just turned and smacked it, and even a keeper of Ray Clemence's ability couldn't get anywhere near it.

By the end I was praying for the final whistle. My legs were like jelly and cramping up, but I still had to jump against John Toshack and he's six foot three and I'm only five foot ten. So when the whistle went I just felt relief, which is a bit sad I suppose. Still, we did the Double and no one can take that away from us, and it was a lot harder to do then than it is now.

39

Northern Ireland 5   Austria 3
European Championship qualifier
Windsor Park, attendance 8,500
16 November 1995

There were more people cheering this game on in the Stadium of Light in Lisbon (where Jack Charlton's Republic were playing the in-form Portugal) than there were at Windsor Park, but the 8,500 hardy souls who were there witnessed an astounding Northern Ireland performance. The Austrians knew that if they won they would be odds-on to qualify for Euro 96. If they lost then the Republic would finish second whatever the result in Portugal. What the Austrians didn't know, and they weren't alone, was that this young Northern Ireland side was capable of tearing them to pieces.

With the rain lashing down and the wind raging, the goals began raining in like they were trying to keep up with the weather. Hibernian star Michael O'Neill scored the first with a left-foot shot in the twenty-seventh minute, and five minutes later it was 2–0 to Northern Ireland thanks to an Iain Dowie penalty. As the Republic fans in Lisbon cheered the news in disbelief, their counterparts in Belfast stared in disbelief as Barry Hunter of Wrexham made it 3–0 early in the second half. The Austrians, who along with Portugal had been the form team in the run-up to the group showdown, pulled one back, but then a Phil Gray goal on sixty-three minutes made it 4–1. This was getting silly. The Austrians clipped in another goal only for O'Neill to get his second with a delightful chip, and not even another Austrian goal at the death could dampen Northern Irish spirits.

The pace and flair his team had shown against a team that wouldn't have looked out of place in England in the summer of 1996 had made Bryan Hamilton justifiably proud. Even Billy Bingham's great Northern Ireland team of the 1980s never scored five – it hadn't happened since Cyprus were trounced 5–0 in 1971. The only sour note on the night was the news that, after the Republic's result in Portugal, Northern Ireland only missed out on second place in the group and an Anfield play-off showdown with Holland by one goal!

I was there . . . Bryan Hamilton

The weather was wild at Windsor Park that night, but from where I was standing believe me the sun was shining! It was a great team performance. We were always in control and we always looked like scoring, in fact I think we really should have stuck a few more away. Austria didn't exactly play badly, but we played ever so well.

Our preparation was good, that's something we'd been working on. We try to give the players plenty to do, to exercise their minds a bit and build up team spirit. Like we had a ten-pin bowling competition the day before, in which Keith Gillespie and I were knocked out in the first round – the lads were out to get us because we won last time. We went around and about in the days before the match, meeting disabled kids, that sort of thing, trying to make an effort to be part of the community. It's important. Our team covers every crack and grain in the community, and we want the whole community to know that, to feel part of what's going on and to come down to Windsor Park to see us play and get behind us. And for the Austria match, in terrible weather, the crowd was fantastic.

To pick a man of the match would be impossible, everyone played so well. The back four, the middle four, the strikers. Afterwards the lads were obviously on a high, but there was a kind of unspoken tinge of regret in the dressing-room when we realized how close we had, in fact, come. It was a case of so near, yet so far.

40

Liverpool 3   Everton 2
(a.e.t. 1–1)
FA Cup final
Wembley Stadium, attendance 82,800
20 May 1989

An FA Cup final where the result didn't matter? Not quite, but the issue of winning or losing on 20 May 1989 was secondary on a day of unrivalled emotion at Wembley.

It was five weeks earlier, during Liverpool's semi-final against Nottingham Forest at Hillsborough, that ninety-five Liverpool fans had died in Britain's worst sporting disaster. The fact that their opponents in the final of a competition so nearly abandoned out of respect for the dead were Merseyside rivals Everton was appropriate. The atmosphere at Wembley was one of togetherness, a city in mourning, a fitting memorial. Inside the stadium the perimeter fencing had been removed and segregation was barely noticeable. Gerry Marsden sang 'You'll Never Walk Alone' in the dazzling May sunshine and there was a deafening minute's silence.

Kenny Dalglish's Liverpool side had vowed to win the Cup in memory of the fans they had lost and after five minutes it looked like it was going to be plain sailing when John Aldridge, who'd missed a penalty against Wimbledon the previous year, put them one up. Liverpool dominated but couldn't add to Aldridge's single strike. Playing some of the best football seen all season, at times it was Liverpool v. Southall with the big Welsh keeper the only man standing between the Reds and a rout. Aldridge could have had a hat-trick and Barnes had more than one good chance to put the game beyond Everton's reach. With twenty-five minutes remaining, Everton boss Colin Harvey brought on Stuart McCall for Paul Bracewell and suddenly they started to pin Liverpool back. From nowhere it was all Everton but they couldn't find a way through until, in the last seconds, McCall pounced on a Grobbelaar fumble, sending the match into extra-time and jubilant Evertonians charging on to the pitch.

Substitute Ian Rush, back from his unhappy 'trouble with Italy is it's like a foreign country' spell at Juventus, came off his unfamiliar position on the bench for Aldridge at the start of extra-time and within minutes of the restart he'd made it 2–1. Controlling a Steve Nicol cross superbly, Rush swivelled and fired a low shot past Southall's left arm. It didn't last long. McCall equalized again, this time with a sensational volley from twenty-five yards and now the crowd was displaying emotion of a different kind. Then, amazingly, with the first period of extra-time coming to an end, Rush did it again, latching on to a John Barnes cross and scoring the winner with a glancing header. This time there was no way back for Everton and the Cup, fittingly, went to Anfield.

It was 3–2 to Liverpool. A memorable match in a year that no football fan could ever forget. The only sour note was the behaviour of a minority of supporters who, with the perimeter fences removed, came on to the pitch during and at the end of the match on this most sensitive of occasions.

I was there . . . Steve McMahon

This is the greatest game I was ever involved in, for obvious reasons. It was a fitting occasion after the tragedy of Hillsborough. It was a special day that at least went some way, however small, towards healing some of the wounds.

The parents and relatives of many of those who'd died at Hillsborough had said that they wanted us to continue in the FA Cup, because they thought that's what they would have wanted. And once we started again in the rearranged semi-final against Forest there was only ever one team that was going to win it.

It was important for us to win the Cup in memory of those who had died, it was everyone's wish, and to do that felt very, very special. The fact that we played Everton in the final, of course, made the whole thing perfect.

41

Arsenal 4   Manchester United 5
League Division One
Highbury, attendance 63,578
1 February 1958

irst a trip to Highbury, then a trip to Belgrade to
defend a slender 2–1 lead in the European Cup: the
future looked good for the Busby Babes, Matt
Busby's refreshing and highly successful young team, in
the new year of 1958. What happened in Munich on the
way back from Belgrade is well chronicled and tragically
sad: the plane carrying the United team crashed taking
off in a snowstorm and twenty-three passengers,
including eight players, were killed. The fact that the
Babes produced a stunning performance days before
the crash only heightens the tragedy in footballing terms.
Not only were lives sadly lost, the most promising football team for decades, one that looked likely to put
England back on the football map, was decimated.

United's side against Arsenal was the same that was
to face Red Star four days later, and they quickly showed
their style. Dennis Viollet laid the ball on to twenty-one-
year-old Duncan Edwards and the left-half whumped in
an unstoppable goal. Then Albert Scanlon ran half the
length of the field to cross for Bobby Charlton, who
smacked in a second. Next another Scanlon run found

Morgans who chipped in for Tommy Taylor to score; 3–0 at half-time and it seemed to be all over.

Fifteen minutes into the second half, though, Arsenal, remarkably, scored three in as many minutes to draw level, through Herd and Bloomfield (two), with the Babes showing some of the defensive naivety that comes with youth. Many teams would have crumbled, or tried to play out a draw, but the Busby Babes went for Arsenal's throat after their three-minute hiccup. Scanlon and Charlton set up Viollet to score, then Tommy Taylor got the last for United, and his last ever. Derek Tapscott pulled it back to 4–5, but Arsenal didn't have time to equalize. Even the Arsenal supporters left the stadium in a state of euphoria.

Five days later the whole country was in mourning. Five of the side that beat Arsenal didn't make it back from Belgrade, including goalscorers Edwards and Taylor. The death of left-half Edwards in particular was a huge loss to English, and world, football. He was a fantastic prospect, with eighteen England caps and five international goals to his name before his twenty-first birthday, a man widely tipped to be the next England captain. At Old Trafford they will never be forgotten . . . nor at Highbury.

42

Of all the places to win the League, Arsenal do it at White Hart Lane. With 50,000 fans locked outside, the Gunners sent their fans into ecstasy with a 1–0 win in a titanic encounter. It was a remarkable night to end a remarkable season. With Don Revie's Leeds seemingly cruising to another title win, Arsenal started stringing together win after win in the title run-in. Meanwhile Leeds stuttered and spluttered, their erratic form coming to a head in the 2–1 home 'offside controversy' defeat by West Brom.

At Arsenal, under Bertie Mee and Don Howe and with Footballer of the Year Frank McLintock solid as a rock at the heart of the defence, a good season was steadily turning into a great one. And when it came to the night of Monday, 3 May, the Gunners needed a goalless draw or a win to clinch the title. That would tie them with Leeds on points but give them the title by virtue of a slender goal average advantage.

It was tense, but it was also fast and exciting. Far from defending for the 0–0, Arsenal went on the attack and Spurs returned the compliment. The Gunners had the better of the match but with two minutes to go it was still 0–0. With a wonderful rising header Ray Kennedy gave Arsenal the lead. The red and white end of the ground went mad but Spurs were soon on the attack, and a Tottenham goal now would still deprive Arsenal of the title. In the dying seconds Bob Wilson risked his good looks (and a future TV career) by diving into a sea of legs to retrieve the ball in an almighty scramble on the Arsenal goal line, and then the whistle blew. Arsenal fans jigged manically on the pitch of their nearest and not so dearest. They'd done it, and even some of the Spurs fans gave them a clap. Well, some.

I was there . . . Bob Wilson

It was unreal. Before the match we couldn't get down the Seven Sisters Road because it was blocked solid with people. The coach literally got stuck two or three hundred yards away from the ground, in the middle of the crowd, and we didn't get to White Hart Lane until about forty-five minutes before the game.

I had all my pre-match preparations that I liked to do: I used to throw a ball against the wall to catch and I even used to shoulder-charge the dressing-room wall to get myself going. I started doing that after I came up against Derek Dougan in the first thirty seconds of a match against Wolves once and I wasn't quite ready for him, and I even cracked the marble on the wall of the dressing-room at Highbury once. Anyway, I remember that none of us had time for our routines, and I think that was good for us. There was less time to think and less time to worry. Of course the north London derby was the biggest game of the season anyway, but to be going to White Hart Lane with a chance of doing the Double, and with Tottenham being the last side to do it, well it was just incredible. The atmosphere was something else, it was extraordinary.

We either needed a win or a 0–0 draw to win the title. Anything else and we'd lost it. A 1–1 draw or a 2–2 draw was no good. It was a tight game but then, with eight minutes to go, Ray Kennedy scored. I remember jumping in the air in celebration, which was quite unlike me, and an Arsenal fan running on the pitch and hugging me.

Then all hell broke loose. It would almost have been better if we hadn't scored because suddenly Spurs were coming at us from all angles. Of course they didn't want Arsenal to win the title on their soil and the last ten minutes were horrendous – if they'd got a goal then we'd've lost it – and I had to dive at Alan Mullery's feet during one wholehearted scramble.

When the whistle blew the Arsenal fans went mad; there were so many on the pitch that I couldn't see any of our players, so I turned round and hugged the nearest person who happened to be the referee. I was jumping up and down and hugging him with blood all over my face, he must have thought I was mad.

We did celebrate – and I remember Bertie Mee taking his jacket off which we'd never seen before – but it was all quite restrained. We knew we had a job to do, and in five days' time we were playing in the Cup final at Wembley.

43

Tottenham 2   Chelsea 1
FA Cup final
Wembley Stadium, attendance 100,000
20 May 1967

This was the first all-London final of the century between two classic sides. Bill Nicholson's Spurs included Pat Jennings, Joe Kinnear, Mike England, Alan Mullery, Cyril Knowles, Alan Gilzean, Jimmy Greaves and Terry Venables, whereas Tommy Docherty's Chelsea boasted the likes of Peter Bonetti, John Hollins, Ron 'Chopper' Harris, Tony Hateley (Mark's dad) and, importantly, Don Mackay, their captain, back after a series of injuries. It was Spurs' third final of the decade, having won the Double in 1961 and retained the Cup in 1962. But with Blanchflower retired and most of the glory gang having moved on, it was high time Spurs won another trophy – and having come close in the Championship, finishing third behind Manchester United and Forest, Tottenham were hungry for success.

'It was a classic match because it was a great Spurs performance,' says Alan Mullery. 'It was much more of a foregone conclusion than the scoreline suggests, a one-horse race.' Tottenham gelled from the start, with Greaves and Gilzean a constant menace up front, and England controlling the back. The only threat that

Chelsea could muster came in the first half through the erratic dribbling skills of Charlie Cooke. Mullery finally broke Chelsea's resolute defending, bursting through the middle with the referee looking at his half-time watch. His shot was blocked, but Robertson picked up the rebound to strike past Bonetti. Midway through the second half, Saul had the cockerels crowing with a spectacular goal, hooking a shot on the turn past Bonetti, the sourpuss 'Cat'. Chelsea's response was too late to make any difference to the result, Tambling gaining scant consolation four minutes from the final whistle. The Blues would have to wait a further five years for their Cup final glory.

I was there . . . John Hollins

What do I remember of the 1967 FA Cup final? I remember that we played Tottenham, they kept the ball for eighty minutes and could have scored five or six.

We were always second best and, in fact, the scoreline flattered us. They had a great team with people like Dave Mackay, Mike England, Alan Mullery and Jimmy Greaves and they passed it around superbly on the Wembley pitch which was absolutely perfect. They moved the ball so well. I played on the right and all I kept seeing was three or four white shirts coming towards me. Wherever we had one player, they seemed to have three. How we kept the score down I don't know. I think they were so in control that by the end they were trying to score the perfect goal, and Peter Bonetti made some great saves to keep the score respectable.

It doesn't make defeat any easier when you know you've been thoroughly beaten, it just makes you think, 'What do we do to get up to this level?' Ironically we got to three semi-finals around then and this was probably the weakest side of the three. This was a truly great Spurs side but we weren't fearful of playing them. But once they'd got on top that was it; even though we scored near the end we really weren't ever in it. I must have been doing something right personally though because I was back three days later playing for England against Spain, my one and only cap. Playing at Wembley twice in a week isn't too bad I suppose, and at least we won that time, 2–0.

44

Benfica 5   Real Madrid 3
European Cup final
Olympic Stadium, Amsterdam, attendance 68,000
2 May 1962

The seventh European Cup final, the sixth featuring Real Madrid, was a thrilling climax to what had been a thrilling competition. Neither team had found reaching the final easy. Real took three matches to defeat Juventus (John Charles et al) in the quarter-finals and Benfica had been lucky to come away from Tottenham with a 1–2 defeat in a storming semi-final second leg at White Hart Lane. Real boasted two players who still make World XIs – Ferenc Puskas and the ageing Alfredo Di Stefano. Benfica, on the other hand, had a quick-fire forward fresh in their line-up who was to become one of the greatest players the world has ever seen, the Mozambique-born Eusebio.

The game has become known as 'the night of the long shots' with both sides finding the target regularly from outside the box. Real went two up through their 'galloping major' Puskas, the first after a sixty-yard dash from his own half, the second a thirty-yard blaster. Within ten minutes, however, Aguas and Cavem had levelled things for the Portuguese champions, who had won the 1961 final against Real's bitter rivals Barcelona.

But Puskas completed a first half hat-trick to give the Spaniards the edge at the interval.

The second half was all Benfica, whose Hungarian manager Bela Guttmann shifted his team around after the interval, managing to nullify the Puskas–Di Stefano partnership. What's more, Real's full-back Casada was injured, and in the days before substitutes he was little more than a passenger making up the numbers in the second period. Benfica's Coluna duly thrashed home another thirty-yarder to equalize just after the hour, and then it was time for Eusebio to take centre stage. On sixty-eight minutes the twenty-year-old ran into the box, was felled by a Real defender, and picked himself up to score coolly from the penalty spot. Ten minutes later he blasted a tapped free kick via a deflection off the Spanish wall to make sure the trophy went back to Lisbon.

'It was an honour for me to be on the same pitch as Di Stefano and Puskas,' said Eusebio, nicknamed the black panther, after the match. 'I can hardly believe this is all happening. It seems like only yesterday that I was a young boy in Mozambique kicking a ball around with my bare feet.' The world was to see a lot more of Eusebio.

45

Portugal 5   North Korea 3
World Cup quarter-final
Goodison Park, attendance 51,000
23 July 1966

Hundreds of fans made the journey from, er, Middlesbrough to Goodison Park to cheer on their North
Korean heroes against Eusebio's Portugal, and the
match that ensued was well worth the journey. Skilful,
fast and always on the attack, the North Koreans had
been adopted by the fanatical north-east fans after
playing their group matches at Ayresome Park. Roared
on by the local crowd they had already beaten Italy,
but with Eusebio looking like the best player in the
tournament Portugal at Goodison was going to be
another matter altogether.

Incredibly, the Koreans were 3–0 up inside the first
twenty minutes. Right from the kick-off they were at
Portugal's throats and within a minute they scored, Pak
Seung Jin driving home after a dazzling move. The Portuguese players didn't know what had hit them and it
got worse, Li Dong-Woon and Yang Sung Kook adding
to the surreal scoreline. It would take something
special to pull Portugal out of this one, but in Eusebio
they had just that. After twenty-eight minutes the great
man had pulled one back, powering past three defenders

in the process, and three minutes before half-time he converted a penalty to make it 3–2 after Torres was sent tumbling in the box.

Now it was the North Koreans' turn to be rattled and, eleven minutes into the second half, Eusebio had equalized. Terrorizing the defence with his exhilarating left-wing runs, three minutes later he'd earned another penalty and it was Eusebio 4 North Korea 3. Eusebio was playing like Pelé with twice the strength and three times the determination and the Koreans, who had at no stage sat back on their lead, just couldn't cope. With twelve minutes left Augusto scored Portugal's fifth from a corner and while Portugal celebrated, Goodison caught its breath and Middlesbrough mourned. The rest of the world acclaimed an unbelievable match.

46

Belgium 4   USSR 3
(full-time score 2–2)
World Cup second round
Nou Camp Stadium, León, Mexico, attendance 32,000
18 June 1986

An unexpected classic. The neat, efficient Russians against the so far disappointing Belgians for a place in the quarter-finals. It wasn't the most enthralling prospect of the summer but it turned out to be an explosive battle in the searing Leon heat.

Belgium had only qualified for the second-round knockout stage as one of the best third-placed teams in the group stages, only narrowly beating Iraq, drawing with Paraguay and losing to hosts Mexico. The USSR, on the other hand, with Ivor Belanov in stunning goal-scoring form, were playing efficient, incisive football and had topped their group, beating Hungary 6–0 and drawing with the much fancied French along the way. They were starting to look like possible winners.

Before the match it looked a formality for the USSR. And with the Russians leading 2–1 thanks to two Belanov strikes to Scifo's fifty-fourth-minute reply for Belgium, with fifteen minutes left on the clock it looked like it was all going to plan. Then, out of the blue, a long ball out of defence suddenly put veteran thirty-year-old Belgian striker Jan Ceulemans in the clear. As the Russian team stood and waited for the offside flag that never came, Ceulemans finished and the match was destined for another enthralling half-hour.

In extra-time the Belgians suddenly and spectacularly hit form and soon found themselves 4–2 up. A far-post header from De Mol and a strike from Nico Claesen had put them in the driving seat. Then, with the Russians pouring forward, Belanov became the first Russian to score a hat-trick in the World Cup finals with a penalty three minutes from the end to set up a rousing finish. But it was not to be, and when Belgian keeper Pfaff just got his hand to a glorious chip by Yevtushenko in the dying seconds, his side were through.

From nowhere Belgium had found their form (now it would take Maradona's Argentina to stop them in the semi-finals) and the steady Russians, who'd looked to be cruising through the tournament, were on their way home. Belgium eventually finished fourth after losing 4–2 to France in an unusually exciting third-place play-off.

47

The 'Hand of God', the guile of Maradona and the head of Lineker... this was a classic. Four years earlier the two countries had been at war. This was a sporting re-run, the first time since the Falklands conflict that the two countries had met on any sporting field. And this time it was Argentina who took the honours.

There wasn't much honour about their first goal at the beginning of the second half though (like many classic matches the first half was memorable only for its dullness). Steve Hodge, trying to clear a speculative Maradona chip at the edge of the box, only succeeded in hoisting the ball over his shoulder into the area. Shilton was slow to react, Maradona was quicker, managing to get a fist to the ball where the goalkeeper, with a badly timed jump, couldn't. The ball ended up in the net, and, although it was clear to everyone in the stadium and the TV audience that a handball had been committed, both linesman and referee missed it and, infamously, on fifty minutes Argentina were ahead. Within four minutes, the lead was doubled. Maradona picked up the ball in the centre circle and with a deft flick beat Beardsley and Reid and accelerated towards goal. Butcher and Fenwick were his next obstacles but he shimmied past them as if they didn't exist, rounded Shilton and, from the tightest of angles and with Butcher steaming in, slipped it into the back of the net.

Bobby Robson brought on Waddle and Barnes for Reid and Steven, and England, with time running out, started to play, with the Argentines dropping back to try to protect their lead. A Hoddle free kick was beaten out by Argentine goalkeeper Pumpido. Then on eighty minutes an electric Barnes got to the by-line, delivered a telling cross and Lineker headed in at the far post to halve the deficit. With three minutes to go an almost identical move saw an almost identical result, but this time Lineker landed in the net and the ball stayed out. He should have used his hand perhaps. It was that sort of day for England, but in terms of chances created Argentina deserved to shade it, as England hadn't had a sniff until the last period when the Argentinians let them attack.

The Tunisian referee, Ali Ben Naseur, by the way, who made the most famous blunder in World Cup history and also conspired to block an English free kick while on the end of the Argentinian wall, has never refereed an international match since.

I was there . . . Kenny Sansom

I think everyone in the world but the referee saw Maradona put the ball in with his hand. I just couldn't believe it. I saw the whole thing from the edge of the box and

I was just waiting to hear the whistle, it didn't cross my mind that he wouldn't blow it. Peter Shilton was furious. He's taken some stick for the goal but he would definitely have got to the ball if Maradona hadn't flicked it with his hand. The thing is, he did it so quickly. Shilts chased the ref all the way to the halfway line, and after the game the players were still incensed, furious. We were all saying that the game should be replayed, it had to be replayed, but of course there was never any chance of that.

As for Maradona's second goal, well that was something special. I was going forward at the time so I saw it all from the halfway line – which the lads commented on afterwards – and all I saw was the back of him running, this number ten steaming down the pitch. You have to say it was special, he knew what he was doing all right, but I reckon Terry Fenwick would have brought him down if he hadn't already been booked.

After that I thought it was all over, I must admit. But after John Barnes came on and Gary got a goal we were back in it, and I reckon if we scored again – which we nearly did: Gary's header only missed by a foot or so – then we'd have gone on to win it.

48

Arsenal 3   Manchester United 2
FA Cup final
Wembley Stadium, attendance 100,000
12 May 1979

There must be a few poor sods, somewhere, who left the stadium with five minutes to go, Arsenal 2–0 up, to avoid the rush. Bad move.

Four minutes to go and Terry Neill made one of the tactical blunders of all time when he put on young substitute Steve Walford for David Price, presumably to give him a winner's medal. When the substitution was made Arsenal had been cruising what would have gone down as a very ordinary final, with Liam Brady the only star on show, and then they completely lost their shape and concentration. 'We were thinking about walking up those steps and being handed our winner's medals by Prince Charles,' said a young David O'Leary after the match. And who could blame them?

Suddenly, on eighty-six minutes, Coppell hit a free kick into the box, Jordan centred and big Scot Gordon McQueen pulled one back. Two more minutes went by, and United, strangely subdued all match, were rampant. Again it was Coppell the provider, this time to Sammy McIlroy, who waltzed past the unfortunate Walford and O'Leary and hit the ball between Jennings and his post.

Arsenal at this point were desperate to take the match to extra-time so they could regain a little composure, even if United had their tails up. But Liam Brady was having none of that sort of thing. Picking the ball up in his own half, surrounded by red United shirts, he saw Graham Rix running free on the left. Rix spotted Alan Sunderland on the far post, and his perfect pass foxed Bailey and the muppet-haired striker was presented with a near-open goal (although he did injure himself in stretching to connect with the ball). Arsenal, dramatically, had snatched it, just when we were all looking forward to another half an hour's football. 'United forgot one of the oldest maxims of the game,' said Bobby Charlton afterwards, 'that you are at your most vulnerable just after you score.'

For the record, in the other match, the boring one in the first eighty-six minutes, Arsenal scored through Talbot and Stapleton and defended with a meanness that stifled United into virtual inactivity. Nelson and Rice blocked the wings, Willie Young and David O'Leary clogged up the middle, Jennings looked ten feet wide in goal. Talbot terriered away in midfield, snapping up anything loose. Both goals, of course, were set up by Liam Brady. Maybe the genial Irishman wrote the script too.

I was there . . . Liam Brady

It was a great game, but only because of what happened in the last five minutes. I don't think there will ever be a final like it again. It's rare enough to see three goals in five minutes at any time in any match, but to get them in the last five minutes of an FA Cup final . . .

We'd ended up playing a counter-attacking game for most of the match. Not by choice, but because after we took the lead in the first half United were always coming at us. But when we went in at half-time 2–0 up we all thought we had at least one hand on the Cup. In the second half they huffed and puffed, and we tried to attack them on the break. We looked pretty comfortable though, and Pat Jennings was on superb form, and we probably should have scored again ourselves – then suddenly all hell broke loose.

When Gordon McQueen scored we lost it. We'd seen the finishing line and we started to panic. In a Cup final you play instinctively, there's no time to think about what you're doing, so instead of keeping the ball we started giving it away. And they scored again. It was such a shock. We'd been five minutes away from a comfortable win, now we didn't know what was going to happen. Would they score again? Would it go to extra-time, when they'd undoubtedly have the psychological advantage?

So from the kick-off I got the ball and I just thought, 'Let's get the bloody ball in their half.' So I ran with it, and as I ran the space just seemed to open up for me, so I kept going. Then Graham Rix came up outside me and I played the ball to him, he played in one of those crosses that the keeper thinks he's going to get but then realizes he isn't, and Alan Sunderland stuck it in. Fantastic. The United players just collapsed to the floor. We'd lost the Cup to Ipswich the year before so the celebrations were even more enjoyable, it was a very proud feeling. But, like I say, I don't think there will ever be a final like it again.

49

Italy 0   North Korea 1
World Cup group four
Ayresome Park, Middlesbrough, attendance 18,000
19 July 1966

Three syllables are enough to bring a blush of shame to the face of any Italian football fan: Pak Doo-ik, the name of the inside-left who scored the goal for North Korea that knocked the Italians out of the World Cup in 1966.

North Korea didn't start the tournament with much hope having been drawn against the USSR, Italy and Chile. Before the tournament they hadn't played any competitive football in Asia, let alone in the World Cup finals. And although the Middlesbrough crowd (they played their group matches at Ayresome) had taken the Asian team to their hearts, they looked completely down and out until two minutes from the end of their second game. The Soviets had brushed them aside 3–0 and then Chile had taken a deserved 1–0 lead seemingly to knock them out of the tournament. But with seconds remaining on the clock against the Chileans, the Ayresome crowd went mad when Pak Seung Zin scored. The Koreans (for whom the word 'plucky' might have been invented) were not finished yet, it seemed.

So it was that 'the diddy men' (as they were

nicknamed) met mighty Italy four days later. In one of the more bizarre selection decisions in the history of the game, Italian coach Fabbri, though knowing that speed was the Asians' main asset, fielded slowpoke defenders Jarnich and Guarneri, as well as the injured Bulgarelli in midfield. On forty-two minutes, with Bulgarelli off the pitch after re-injuring his knee fouling an opponent, Pak Doo-ik dispossessed Rivera and advanced on the Italian goal. It might have been a cross that accidentally beat goalkeeper Albertosi that day, it might have been a brilliantly placed shot, but the end result was the same. And try as they might, Italy couldn't equalize and went out of the World Cup.

The story doesn't quite end there. North Korea had earned themselves a place in the quarter-final, and were pitted against mighty Portugal. After amazingly going three goals up, an incredible place in the semi-finals looked on the cards. Alas, it was not to be.

Italy, for their part, knew what fate was to befall them, and when they got off their plane in Italy they were met by a huge and angry crowd who pelted them with rotten fruit, vegetables, in fact just about anything that came to hand.

50

Holland 2   USSR 0
European Championship final
Olympic Stadium, Munich, attendance 72,000
25 June 1988

Holland's first major international honour took a long
time coming, but it was well worth the wait. Rinus
Michels's classic 'total football' side of the mid-
1970s had been pipped at the final post in the 1974
World Cup final and the Cruyffless 1978 team had been
beaten in the following tournament by a Kempes-
inspired Argentina. But this time Holland, again
managed by Michels, weren't facing the competition
hosts in a major final as they had disposed of Germany
– sweet revenge – in the semi. The USSR were their
opponents, a team which had beaten them in the
opening game of the qualifying group.

This was the Holland side of the great Milan triumvirate – Rijkaard, Gullit and van Basten – which also
included Koeman and the evergreen Arnold Muhren.
The Russians meanwhile included the dangerous Mikhail-
ichenko, Zavarov and Belanov in their ranks.

Marco van Basten was the real star of the day, and
the best player of the tournament, spearheading Holland's attack with ruthless determination and
breathtaking skill. And it was van Basten who rose above

the Soviets and headed a cross back into the centre for his dreadlocked partner in crime Ruud Gullit to head home for a deserved lead on thirty-three minutes. Eight minutes after the break, van Basten produced a piece of brilliance that will live in the memory for years. Muhren's lobbed pass fell to the Milan striker wide of the far post. He would have done well just to control the ball, or knock it back across goal. Instead he unleashed a fierce right-foot volley between the startled Soviet keeper and his left-hand post. It was the fifth goal by van Basten, and the best by anyone in the tournament.

The Soviets, to their credit, came out to attack after this, and after fifty-seven minutes van Breukelen recklessly gave away a penalty. Belanov hit it, the Dutch keeper blocked. If any country deserved to break their trophy duck it was Holland, and this side could have lived with their illustrious 1970s predecessors.

51

AC Milan 5   Real Madrid 0
European Cup semi-final
San Siro Stadium, attendance 73,112
19 April 1989

Milan fans were cursing their luck when the 1989 European Cup semi-final draw was announced. They could have got Galatasaray or Steaua Bucharest. Instead they were drawn against mighty Real Madrid, champions of Spain.

Having scraped through the two previous matches, against tough opponents Red Star Belgrade (on penalties after two 1–1 draws) and Werder Bremen (1–0 on aggregate) they deserved an easier draw. A 1–1 tie in the Bernabeu set Milan up as favourites to squeeze through, but nobody expected the type of dominating performance that was to thrill the San Siro crowd that night.

Milan were superb, with midfielders Ancelotti and Rijkaard and front men van Basten and Gullit dominating, the play was almost entirely fought out in the Spaniards' half. Beenhaker's Real were no pushovers though – this was the era of Butragueño, Martin Vasquez, Schuster and Michel – and had come to Milan with an attacking formation, looking for a win. But they hardly got a look-in after Ancelotti netted the opener on eighteen minutes, blasting a twenty-five-yarder past the surprised Buyo. Real were shell-shocked and after a series of corners Rijkaard headed in a Tassotti cross. The San Siro crowd couldn't believe it: 2–0 up with only twenty-five minutes gone. On the stroke of half-time they'd wrapped things up when Donadoni exchanged passes with Gullit before crossing for the dreadlocked Dutchman to head home.

The tune didn't change in the second half. Real, the life beaten out of them, were a ghost of a team, shown once and for all that their best days were behind them. Van Basten calmly added a fourth from Gullit's header on forty-nine minutes, and ten minutes later Donadoni's shot crept in between the post and the goalkeeper. At this point it looked like Milan only had to shoot to score. There was, however, a blackspot: Gullit hobbled off on the hour with an injured knee that was to require carti-lage surgery, to be replaced by elder statesman Virdis. If he could have played on, the score would almost cer-tainly been even more embarrassing for Real.

The 73,000 San Siro crowd was in raptures, so happy that they even applauded when they heard the news that Napoli and Sampdoria had drawn and won to get through to the finals of the Uefa and Cup Winners' cups. Italian football was indisputably top of the European pile, and Milan were without doubt the best team the continent had seen for a long, long while. Juan 'Pepe' Schiaffino, the former Uruguayan inside-forward and one of Milan's biggest heroes of all time after his exploits in the great 1960s *Rossoneri* side, watched the match as part of the Uruguay party in Milan for a forthcoming friendly against Italy. After the game he said: 'This is a stupendous Milan side. But even more stupendous was the crowd. I'm so pleased I came because these people have, in one blow, taken twenty years off my life.' Gianni Rivera, himself a former AC Milan star, added: 'It's a long time since I've felt such emotion at a football match. It was like when I was playing, perhaps even better. Tonight's Milan were really reminiscent of the side that won the European Cup some twenty years ago. How I would have liked to have been playing.'

52

Ajax 4   Bayern Munich 0
European Cup quarter-final, first leg
Olympic Stadium, Amsterdam, attendance 52,000
7 March 1973

In a second half in which 'total football' totally demolished Bayern Munich, Johan Cruyff's breathtaking
Ajax played possibly the best football of their three-
year reign as European champions.

With the score goalless at half-time, Ajax came out
and blitzed the Bayern side of Beckenbauer and Muller
with a display of football which had the purists purring.
Swarming around Maier's goal, attacking with incisive
sweeping movements and finishing without mercy, this
was Cruyff, Rep, Krol, Neeskens et al at their brilliant
best. The Ajax system required a team of skilful all-
rounders whose versatility and football intelligence
allowed for breathtaking flexibility and bewildering
changes of position. And Ajax had those players. Goals
from Arnold Muhren's brother Gerrie, Arie Haan and
Johan Cruyff gave Ajax a convincing lead in the first leg
in the Olympic Stadium in Amsterdam. The second-
half performance was football poetry, the passing, the
movement and the finishing unsurpassable. Bayern were
demolished and despite a 2–1 reverse in the return in

Munich Ajax made it to their third European Cup final in a row.

In the final they made it a triple of wins by beating Juventus 1–0 thanks to Johnny Rep's fourth-minute strike, though the scoreline didn't reflect the Dutch club's domination. It was the pinnacle of three years of breathtaking European domination and only now is the club coming out of the shadows of that great team, although everything it has achieved in recent years has been based on the very same principles of the 1970s.

53

Charlton 7   Huddersfield 6
League Division Two
The Valley, attendance 12,535
21 December 1957

Charlton cursed their luck when, after fifteen minutes of this pre-Christmas match, they were down to ten men. Derek Ufton broke his collarbone, and this was well before the age of substitutes. Huddersfield capitalized, scoring two goals before half-time against the beleaguered Robins, through Massey and Bain.

At that stage the score seemed pretty normal to the crowd, which was smaller than usual due to the last-minute Christmas shoppers. But things were to go completely barmy in the second half. Within ten minutes of the restart Huddersfield scored three more through Bain, McGarry and Ledger. Charlton only managed a solitary reply, through Summers, just after the break. 1–5 after fifty-five minutes, and not a very happy Valley – indeed hundreds of disgruntled supporters left the ground at this point, fearing further humiliation. They missed half an hour of utter joy.

There were twenty-eight minutes remaining when Charlton left-winger Johnny Summers, thirty, a journeyman forward with his fourth club, decided to play the game of his life, wearing a new pair of boots that he had yet to break in properly. He only put them on in the interval. The old comic hero Billy's Boots would have been impressed by the transformation. The left-footed wideman had scored a hat-trick within six minutes, then added another on eighty-one minutes, all with his 'wrong' right foot, to put Charlton 6–5 up.

The scriptwriter from hell hadn't yet finished. With four minutes to go Huddersfield equalized through Howard, and everybody was preparing to go home, satisfied that neither side had deserved to lose. Summers hadn't finished either. With seconds remaining he put Ryan through to score a last-gasp (and there had been many) goal for Charlton. The referee didn't have the heart to restart the match and blew the final whistle before anything else could happen.

Several records were broken that day. Huddersfield are the only team to have scored six goals and lost, the 7–6 scoreline still being unique in Football League history. There must be some Charlton fans, somewhere, who are still cursing their luck for having stomped out early.

54

Zaïre 2   Zambia 2
(full-time score 1–1)
African Nations Cup final
International Stadium, Cairo, attendance 950
12 March 1974

Everything about life in Zambia and Zaïre was on the up in 1974. Their economies were relatively strong, the standard of living was good . . . and soccer was thriving. So when the two neighbouring nations and great rivals met in the final of the African Nations Cup in 1974, it wasn't just about football but two strong countries fighting for pride. Many expected a classic, but because the Egyptian team – the strong pre-tournament favourites – had been knocked out in the semi-finals by Zambia, it didn't capture the imagination of the people of Cairo. So, bizarrely, the match was played in front of fewer than 1,000 spectators in the vast International Stadium where there was room for another 119,000.

If 120,000 had turned up, however, the match would have disappointed very few of them. It was an even, fast and skilful game with both sides attacking with pace and power. Zaïre took the lead twice, once in normal time and once in extra-time, and both times Zambia came back. The man of the match was undoubtedly the Zaïrean striker Ndaye, and with three minutes of extra-time gone the tournament's top scorer looked to have won the trophy with his second goal of the game. With seconds to go, however, Zambia's Sinyangwe forced the first-ever replay in the history of the African Nations Cup. Even fewer people turned up to see the rematch two days later, and this time Zambia couldn't come back from a double strike by Ndaye and it finished 2–0.

55

Scotland 3   Holland 2
World Cup qualifying round, group four
Mendoza, Argentina, attendance 40,000
11 June 1978

It had been a disaster from beginning to end . . . and then along came Archie Gemmill. Ally's Army (of 'we're on the march with' fame) had been stuffed by Peru and held to a 1–1 draw by Iran. Willie Johnstone had been sent home after failing a drugs test and the local media had branded the team a bunch of heavy drinkers. Now all Scotland had to do was go out and beat just about the best team in the tournament by three clear goals and they'd be through to the next round. And they nearly bloody did it.

Scotland started like a different team from the one the world had seen so far. Bruce Rioch hit the post in the opening five minutes and the Scots were rampant. Normal service was soon resumed, it seemed, when Rensenbrink put the eventual finalists 1–0 up from the penalty spot in the thirty-fourth minute. It looked like more gloom for Scotland, and only made what happened in the next half an hour even more extraordinary.

Continuing to play like a much improved shadow of their former selves, however, Scotland were soon back in it. First Kenny Dalglish levelled the scores just before half-time with a thumping half-volley from Joe Jordan's knockdown, then, seven minutes after the break, Gemmill netted a penalty to make it 2–1. The excitement must have gone to Gemmill's head because, with twenty minutes to go, he had a rush of blood to the head, decided he was Johan Cruyff, and scored the goal of the tournament. Picking up the ball on the edge of the box Gemmill darted towards goal, danced round three bemused defenders and lifted the ball exquisitely past Jongbloed in the Dutch goal. When asked before the game if he thought the Scots could score the three goals they required, Jongbloed had replied: 'Yes, but not in ninety minutes.' He was nearly made to pay for his flippancy.

With the score at 3–1 a miracle was now well and truly on the cards and, for the first time in two weeks, the Scotland fans had something to suggest that perhaps there was at least a faint glimmer of sanity in Ally McLeod's 'We'll win the World Cup' pre-tournament rallying cry. Very faint. Four minutes later it was all over when Johnny Rep, so often Holland's saviour with that lethal left foot, picked up the ball and smashed it in from thirty yards. And to think, it could have been a Scotland v. Argentina final.

I was there . . . Archie McPherson

I'll never forget Archie Gemmill's goal. In my entire career as a commentator I've never seen a whole press box full of reporters and commentators rise up and cheer a goal like they did that night. It was like cheering on a horse to the finish. He picked up the ball and made his way into the box, beating two players and then a third, then checked, hit it with his left, and it was in. Journalists from all over the world were on their feet. Suddenly it looked like they might achieve the impossible. For the first time in the tournament, Scotland were in the World Cup. It didn't last long, however, and I remember the shattering anti-climax of Johnny Rep's goal almost as clearly as Gemmill's strike.

I think the Scotland players just relaxed. After the games against Peru and Iran I think they were just glad that they were getting the hell out of there. I think they'd all got carried away with Ally McLeod's misguided optimism, and by the time it got to the Holland match the mood in the camp was like there'd been a death in the family. I personally hadn't been expecting much from Scotland. I felt that there were too many players who'd passed their peak, like Rioch and Masson. But with Souness and Dalglish coming into the side for the Dutch game and with nothing to lose, suddenly they looked a team worthy of the setting – the Mendoza stadium is a beautiful ground with the Andes rising up behind it. Of course it wasn't to be. Johnny Rep's strike put paid to that, but this match and Gemmill's goal – which earned him the Goal of the Tournament award which was later presented to him by Franz Beckenbauer at Hampden Park – are my enduring memories of the 1978 World Cup. It was certainly better than Scotland's first game against Peru when I turned up and there was no phone line for me so I couldn't do my commentary back to Scotland. My wife was scared that I'd been kidnapped by Argentinian guerrillas; mind you some of my critics were hoping I had!

56

Fifa, in their ultimate wisdom, decided that the 1974 World Cup finals tournament should have no semi-finals, with two round robin groups instead. But with both teams having beaten both their opponents this was, in effect, a semi-final in disguise. Holland had a vastly superior goal difference, so in effect Brazil needed to win: the Dutch could satisfy themselves with a draw.

With Johan Cruyff having taken over the 'world number one' spot and Holland quite palpably the best attacking side of the tournament, the match had a look of a handing-over-of-power. The Brazilians were still of course world champions but in reality weren't half the side they'd been four years earlier. No Pelé, of course: he'd retired and was now working for Pepsi Cola. No Gerson either, nor Tostão or Cloadaldo, injured pre-tournament. Not a hell of a lot of spark and invention, either: this was a brutally defensive Brazil side, harshly criticized by press, ex-pros and fans alike. But it seemed they had to come out and attack if they were to beat Holland, so inventive going forward, so potentially frail in defence, despite their clean goals-against record in the tournament.

Remarkably this wasn't the case. The Brazilians came to harry Holland, not to outwit them, and they hacked and kicked the Dutch from the start; the Dutch, showing that total football could include some negative aspects of the game, responded in kind. Brazil did break down their opponents' offside trap twice in the first half, but first Paolo Cesar then Jairzinho were wasteful in the one-on-one with the goalkeeper.

Unsurprisingly it was a foul, rather than a flash of brilliance, that turned the match. Johan Neeskens was knocked cold by Mario Marinho in the first half, then booted by Pareira, who was sent off for his sins. The extra man gave the Dutch the advantage, and we started to see what magic they were capable of. Neeskens got his own back by scoring after a long-range one-two with Cruyff, lobbing the return superbly over the keeper. Then Cruyff himself got on the score sheet with a cracking volley from Ruud Krol's left-wing centre to make sure of the result. Holland were in the final, Brazil, the doghouse.

57

Italy 0   England 4
Friendly
Studio Communale, Turin, attendance 85,000
16 May 1948

England have had some famous victories, but this must rate as one of their most incredible performances. Against the rampant, super-confident world champions, Italy, and in front of 85,000 screaming fans in the Communale Stadium, Matthews, Finney, Lawton and Mortensen dazzled and made sure it was the quietest night in Turin for years.

But it needed one of the greatest goals England have ever scored to set them on their way and silence the crowd. Matthews picked up the ball from Wright, feinted and jinked his way past two defenders and then, instead of charging down the wing as usual, played the ball left-footed inside to his Blackpool team-mate Stan Mortensen. Mortensen took the ball in his stride and sprinted through the Italian defence towards the by-line. Just outside the box and only a few yards in from the line, with an Italian defender diving at the ball, he turned and unleashed a wonder shot that flashed inside the near post and crashed into the roof of the net.

At half-time it was 2–0 thanks to the heroics of keeper Frank Swift and a goal from Tommy Lawton. In the second half the Italians pressed and pressed but couldn't beat Swift, then another brilliant move that started from the back and ended with Tom Finney rounding the keeper made it 3–0. Italy were beaten. And when Finney added another, they were humiliated.

I was there . . . Tom Finney

Italy were the World Cup holders at this time, even though they won it back in 1938, and hot favourites for this match. They were a tremendous, skilful side and I think the team that day included about eight of the Torino side killed in the terrible air crash the following year.

For the first half an hour it was Italy at their peak, they were all over us. But we defended well and big Frank Swift in goal kept us in the game. Then we scored, against the run of play, and it completely stunned the crowd. Stan Mortensen picked up the ball on the left and started charging down the wing, where he shouldn't have been at all. He practically got to the by-line and looked like he was going to cross it, but then he suddenly hit it and it flew into the net. We were all laughing about it in the dressing-room, saying it was a fluke, but he said he saw the keeper coming out for the cross and I'm sure he did.

A few minutes later Tommy Lawton scored, and at half-time it was 2–0 even though we were lucky to be in front at all. In the second half, though, we came out and really played some great stuff. We ran them ragged really, it was a tremendous victory. I scored a couple of goals in the second half, both times I was put through after a great build-up. It was a truly great team, with men like Matthews, Lawton, Mortensen and Mannion, and a great win.

58

England 2   Portugal 1
World Cup semi-final
Wembley Stadium, attendance 94,000
26 July 1966

The whole of England was abuzz with expectation: Alf Ramsey's team had qualified for the quarter-finals of the 1966 World Cup with the minimum of fuss, and had beaten the 'animals of Argentina' to get through to the semis. A place in the final beckoned . . . but first they had to get past what Bobby Charlton calls 'the best Portuguese side in the country's history' with a player in the ranks who was undoubtedly amongst the world's best, Eusebio. 'We knew that was going to be hard,' says Charlton, 'but we still thought we could beat them; we had a history of good results against Portuguese sides, at club and international level.'

The Portuguese had had a fright on their way to the semi, going 3–0 down to the 'diddy men' of North Korea before winning through 5–3, and had shown a nasty side in their character by resorting to thuggery to get over the Brazilian obstacle in one of their group matches. But they had won all their four matches in the tournament so far, scoring fifteen goals to England's five, and the match was billed as the world's best attack versus the world's best defence.

It was badly billed, as it happened, as the game which ensued was an end-to-end affair serving up numerous chances for both teams. 'It was the best match of the competition. It was end-to-end, it was fast, it was clean,' says Charlton, who was to be the game's main protagonist. And, in the light of what had preceded it, it was an incredibly pure game, played in the most gentlemanly fashion, yielding a total of only ten free kicks in the whole ninety minutes. The match swung both ways before the opening goal on thirty minutes. Goalkeeper Pereira made a bit of a hash of a clearance after Hunt's shot and the ball fell to Charlton who, despite a scrum of bodies between him and the goal, threaded the ball into the net. The score remained 1–0 until half-time, despite a number of England chances inspired by the dynamic running of Alan Ball, and some quickfire attacking by Eusebio and co.

The Portuguese came out in the second half determined to peg one back, but for all their skill and endeavour they couldn't get past the brick wall put up by Jack Charlton, Bobby Moore, Nobby Stiles and Gordon Banks. And in the end it was England who got the second goal, a thumper by Bobby Charlton, who ran on to a sublimely weighted Geoff Hurst pass. If there hadn't been a net in the goal, somebody in the crowd might have been killed. Portugal responded with a Eusebio penalty on eighty-two minutes after Jack Charlton had handled on the line, and then threw caution to the wind, creating a couple of chances that stayed out of the net thanks to brave defending by Stiles and great goal-keeping by Banks. Relief was the first emotion for the English fans, then joy. Eusebio cried; so did Jack Charlton, for God's sake. England were in the World Cup final.

59

England 1   Poland 1
World Cup qualifier
Wembley Stadium, attendance 100,000
17 October 1973

The bare facts of this chill October night were that England had to beat Poland to reach the World Cup finals in Germany. Manager Sir Alf Ramsey let loose the dogs of war, naming an unchanged side from the one that had recently whumped Austria 7–0 in a Wembley friendly, with a formidable front line of Mick Channon, Martin Chivers and Allan 'Sniffer' Clarke. Poland, all in red, were missing the world-class striker Lubarski (who was replaced by the unknown Domarski, to English sighs of relief) but included in their side the bald-headed Lato, the influential Deyna, the thuggish Gorgon and, importantly, a goalkeeper by the name of Tomaszewski who Brian Clough famously dubbed 'The Clown'.

On the night the clown, inevitably, played out of his skin. England dominated the match, raging around the Polish box with mounting urgency, perhaps too much urgency. Channon hit a post, Currie headed over, Tomaszewski saved marvellously from Bell, Clarke and Channon. The first half ended goalless, but it looked a matter of time before England were to break the deadlock. England continued the siege in the second half, bombarding the Polish box with shot after shot. Then, disastrously, Poland mounted a rare attack and capitalized on a clutch of England defensive errors to score. Norman 'bites yer legs' Hunter was left chomping thin air as he missed a tackle on Lato down the right, trying to be clever instead of hoofing the ball into touch. Lato's ball found Domarski, who shot through Hughes's legs. Shilton, somehow, failed to save (he later admitted he was trying to be too flash) and England's task was doubled. Six minutes later England won a dubious penalty when Martin Peters was brought down on the edge of the area. Clarke, nervous as hell, stepped up to score on sixty-three minutes. After that a series of near-goals were kept out by bad luck, bad shooting, or brilliant keeping by Tomaszewski, who looked like he was doing an impression of a brilliant keeper pretending to be a bad keeper, but getting between the ball and the goal anyway. Chivers was replaced by Hector with two minutes remaining (Ramsey had never quite mastered the art of substitution) and the Derby striker's header from England's twenty-third corner (his first touch of the match) was cleared off the line, Clarke stabbing the rebound wide. It simply wasn't England's night, and they were to go out of the competition having thoroughly dominated proceedings, making thirty-five goalscoring chances to Poland's two.

Lord George Wigg said afterwards: 'It's worse than losing a war, a national crisis of the highest magnitude.' Poland, lucky on the night, went on to prove their worth by finishing third in Germany. It wasn't Sir Alf Ramsey's last match in charge of the England team, but the defeat sounded the death knell for the country's most successful manager, who was eventually sacked at the end of the season. Things were to get a lot worse before they got better again.

I was there . . . Colin Bell

The Poland match was my biggest disappointment in football. I was a regular in the side and I was at my prime. This was my World Cup chance. I'd been to Mexico in 1970 but I was on the bench most of the time.

We absolutely paralysed Poland. I think they were in our half once in the whole match and they scored; 90 per cent of the game was played in their eighteen-yard box. They had one shot and scored while we had countless efforts that were saves, hit the post or the bar or just went wide. The keeper made a couple of saves from me, he made a couple from near enough every player in the whole team. If it had been a boxing match the towel would've been thrown in.

Afterwards we were devastated. You don't get more than one or two bites at the cherry when it comes to World Cups and this was my last chance. It was in my system for weeks if not months afterwards, I couldn't let it go. With a bad defeat in the League or something it might last for a couple of days, but this was something completely different. It stayed with me for weeks, it was terrible.

IT WAS MAGIC

I was there . . . Malcolm Allison

What can you say. The goalkeeper was brilliant and Norman Hunter made the kind of mistake that he wouldn't make for another ten years, although Sir Alf Ramsey thought Shilton should have saved the shot.

The crowd was hyped up for the match, the whole country was hyped up, it was the most important game at Wembley for years. I was watching from the TV studio at Wembley with Brian Clough where we were working for ITV, and we were yelling and screaming, but it was one of those games where suddenly you were in the middle of the second half and you realized you were running out of time. Brian had seen Tomaszewski in a game before and had called him 'The Clown'; well he was a super clown! It was just one of those games. In the match in Poland Bobby Moore had made a rare mistake when he'd tried to beat a player and he'd got it off him and stuck it in the net. They had become a jinx team.

But even after they'd scored I thought we'd get back into it. We had so many chances but none of them seemed to be clear-cut. The crowd was willing the ball to go in and, after the penalty, the last ten minutes were about as frantic a ten minutes as you'll ever see.

Afterwards the country was shocked. It was probably England's worst result at Wembley since Hungary in 1953, and I've never seen Sir Alf as upset as he was that night.

60

Czechoslovakia 2   West Germany 2
(a.e.t., 5–3 on penalties)
European Championship final
Belgrade, attendance 45,000
20 June 1976

With the Czechs playing free-flowing, powerful football and the Germans as skilful and resilient as ever, it was an epic contest.

The Czechs, who'd denied England a place in the two-legged quarter-finals by winning qualifying group one, looked to be cruising when they went 2–0 up in twenty-five minutes. Inspired by the skilful Masny and switching the ball all over the pitch brilliantly, the Czech team were good value for their two-goal advantage. But the Germans had been 2–0 down in their semi-final and had overturned the deficit. It only took three minutes for West Germany to get back in the game, Gerd Muller, as ever, leading from the front.

For the next hour the game flowed from end to end, both sides defending and attacking with style and guile. It looked like the Czechs were holding out, until with two minutes to go Holzenbein rose to meet Bonhof's corner and suddenly it was 2–2. The Czechs claimed their keeper had been fouled but the goal stood and West Germany had dragged themselves off the floor in yet another vital game.

In extra-time the weary players tried to conjure a goal from somewhere. The Czechs looked the more likely to score as they had throughout the match, but the Germans hung on and it went to penalties. The first seven spot kicks were on target but someone had to miss, and it was West Germany's Uli Hoeness who poked his over the bar, à la Waddle, to give Czechoslovakia the chance to take the title. Up stepped Panenka to take the kick that would win the trophy for the Czechs. Panenka ran up to the ball, stalled, saw Sepp Maier dive to his left, and coolly chipped the ball right into the middle of the goal where the keeper had just been standing. It was the cheekiest moment of the tournament, and it was enough to win the game. It was the first time a major tournament had been settled by a penalty shoot-out; unfortunately it was not to be the last.

61

Liverpool 3   Inter Milan 1
European Cup quarter-final, first leg
Anfield, attendance 55,000
6 March 1965

'**W**e have been beaten before,' said legendary Inter coach Helenio Herrera after this supercharged night at Anfield, 'but tonight we were defeated.'

It was Liverpool's first season in the European Cup and they beat Anderlecht and FC Koln on the way to facing the mighty Inter Milan. Two hours before kick-off the gates to the Kop were locked and 25,000 heaved and roared for nearly four unforgettable hours on the famous old terrace. Liverpool had won the FA Cup the week before the match and with the Kop chanting to see the trophy, the wily Bill Shankly sent the Inter Milan side out first . . . followed by the injured Milne and Byrne to parade the Cup. The Kop went wild and the Inter players, who had gone over to the Kop end, quickly retreated to the relative sanctuary of the Anfield Road.

The atmosphere was incredible and Liverpool tore straight into the Italians, Roger Hunt scoring against the finest defence in the world in the first few minutes. Mazzola pulled one back for Inter but the Ians, Callaghan and St John, smashed a goal each, and there weren't too many clubs capable of putting three past this Inter team.

In the second leg, however, Inter scored three themselves and Liverpool couldn't reply. Years later the *Sunday Times* uncovered evidence that the referee had been bribed, as Shankly had always claimed.

I was there . . . Ian St John

We were fated to win this match. We'd won the FA Cup the week before, the first time Liverpool had ever done it, and everyone in the city wanted to be at the game. They were queuing up from lunchtime.

It was the best atmosphere you could ever imagine at a League ground; I wouldn't say it was total hysteria but it wasn't far off. The joy of the occasion was incredible, and when Bill Shankly sent the boys out with the Cup the place went mad. The Inter players knew what a redhot atmosphere was like, but I reckon even they must have thought this was something special.

In the match I remember we played out of our skins, we scored three but it should have been four or five. Having won the Cup and with the atmosphere as it was, we played superbly. Unfortunately we made one fatal mistake and Mazzola scored, and that was the goal that was to cost us dear. In the return match in the San Siro the atmosphere was pretty intense too, and we were up against a bent referee as well, as was later proved. It turned out that Inter had been buying referees for years, making sure they had everything they needed, so we were really up against it. We knew it was bad when

we couldn't even get a throw-in! Even so, if we hadn't
let that one goal in at Anfield I don't think even a bought
ref could have helped them.

62

Werder Bremen 5   Anderlecht 3
European Champions League
Weserstadion, Bremen, attendance 32,000
8 December 1993

undesliga champions Werder Bremen became the
first German team to make it into the Champions
League by winning two tough preliminary ties on
aggregate, against Dinamo Minsk and Levski Sofia,
scoring nine goals in the process. By half-time in their
first group match, however, they were probably wishing
they hadn't.

0–3 down against Belgian top dogs Anderlecht in
their match of a tough Champions League group (which
also included Porto and AC Milan), they produced a
stunning second-half performance to leave the country
optimistic about their chances of qualifying for the semis.
It all started so badly for the seaport team, who looked
completely out of their depth at the break. Philippe
Albert (soon to be a Geordie) opened the scoring for the
Belgians on sixteen minutes, and by half-time Anderlecht
were cruising. If they'd known what was going to happen
in the second half they would probably have refused to
leave the dressing-room.

It may have taken Bremen sixty-six minutes to score,
but once they found the target they knew the range.

Rufer and Bratseth reduced the deficit in a fine fightback, but with ten minutes on the clock they were still a goal behind. Then the home crowd went crazy as Hobsch scored to make it 3–3 on eighty-one minutes. And things were to get even better. On eighty-three minutes Bode put them 4–3 up and then Rufer got his second in the last minute to cap a thrilling team performance, and complete the most comprehensive comeback in the history of the European Cup.

Bremen, fired by the turnaround, nearly held Milan at the San Siro in the next match, but were eventually beaten 2–1, and a 5–0 home defeat by Porto put an end to their trophy hopes. Milan went on to thrash Barcelona in the final.

63

Real Madrid 3   AC Milan 2
(a.e.t. 2–2)
European Cup final
Heysel Stadium, Brussels, attendance 70,000
29 May 1958

This tournament was overshadowed by the tragic
Munich air crash which decimated Sir Matt Busby's
Manchester United, the most promising side
England had produced for years. Milan got to the final
by beating the shattered remnants of that side 5–2 on
aggregate. Real, meanwhile, had steamrolled their way
through to the final, scoring twenty-four goals in three
matches. It was their third consecutive final, and they
started as big favourites over the Italians, captained by
the great Swede Nils Liedholm.

Real's best player was the Argentinian Alfredo Di
Stefano, 'the white arrow', who was, as ever, hugely
influential on the day. He scored Real's first goal and
played a part in the other two. Di Stefano played from
box to box (and we're talking six-yard box), marshalling
his men into action and leading by example, a total
footballer before the birth of total football.

Nevertheless, Real were trailing twice in the match,
first to a goal by Uruguayan inside-forward Juan Schiaffino on fifty-nine minutes. Then the match soared into
a peak of excitement with a flurry of three goals in five

minutes: Di Stefano equalized on seventy-four, Grillo responded for Milan on seventy-eight, and a minute later another Real goal took the match into extra-time. Gento won the game for the Spaniards as the seconds ticked away.

Di Stefano was undoubtedly the best player in the world at the time, and Real's success in the competition was helped by his ten goals in only seven starts. He was captain of perhaps the greatest-ever club side. It was the Madrileños' third European Cup victory in a row, and the third of five consecutive successes.

64

Scotland 2   Czechoslovakia 1
World Cup qualifier
Hampden Park, attendance 100,000
26 September 1973

his was a night when a 100,000-strong tartan army roared Scotland into the World Cup finals in Germany. All the tickets sold out within days, and the match was transmitted live to a transfixed nation. After beating Denmark both home and away, the Scots were through if they could beat the Czechs at Hampden. And with their final game an away tie in Czechoslovakia it was all or nothing, do or die.

What a battle it was. First Dalglish and then Hutchison were up-ended, then Denis Law marked his return to international football with a dreadful lunge at Bendl. As the crowd chanted 'animals' at the Czechs, Bremner entered into the spirit of the occasion and clattered into Khuna who was too badly injured to continue. Amidst the mayhem, Scotland attacked with Bremner, Jardine and Morgan all going close. Then, disaster, as the Czechs scored. Nehoda swiped at a hopeful punt upfield but Hunter in the Scottish goal flapped and the ball crept in. Silence.

But the quiet didn't last long. Playing fast, attacking football, the Scots increased the pressure and when Manchester United's Jim Holton headed the equalizer from a Tommy Hutchison corner Hampden Park exploded. It was going to get noisier. With Law and Coventry's Hutchison terrorizing the Czech goal a winner always looked likely, but the Czechs looked dangerous on the break and the match was precariously balanced. Scotland pressed and pressed but nothing came of it, so manager Willie Ormond played his trump card – big Joe Jordan. He came on to replace Dalglish and immediately his sheer presence unsettled the Czech defence. One Jordan header flew just over the bar and the crowd raised the noise level even higher, the adrenalin was in full flow. With fifteen minutes remaining Bremner fired in a blistering shot which smacked against a post and rolled agonizingly along the line and past the other. Willie Morgan was the first to react; he chipped the ball back, and Jordan was there to rocket his header into the back of the net. Pandemonium. Czechoslovakia piled men forward in the frantic last minutes but Scotland held out and a place in Germany the following summer was booked. Scotland were the first team to qualify and the players were carried shoulder-high by the ecstatic crowd.

'Every player on that pitch played above themselves that night,' recalls Billy Bremner, who ran the show from the heart of the Scottish midfield. 'It was one of those nights when the Hampden crowd was just unbelievable and it raised the whole team on to a higher level. I'll never forget it.'

65

Romania 3   Argentina 2
World Cup second round
Pasadena Rose Bowl, Los Angeles, attendance 90,000
3 July 1994

With the banned Maradona in the press box, causing as much havoc as he had among opposition defences earlier in the tournament, Romania and Argentina served up the finest match of the 1994 World Cup. And when the TV cameras cut away from the madman in the stands, they homed in on three superb Romanian goals.

Diego-less Argentina, marshalled by the impressive Redondo, played the sweeping attacking football that had made them look possible winners of the tournament, but Romania's classy counter-attacking more than matched them. Dumitrescu opened the scoring early in front of 90,000 fans in the Rose Bowl with a free kick special. Five minutes later Batistuta put the Argentinians level from the penalty spot but Maradona's joy was short-lived. Two minutes after the equalizer Hagi swept downfield, provided the perfect ball for Dumitrescu and his precise finish was to do wonders for his chances of an overseas transfer.

Argentina dominated the match from here on, pressing and probing for an equalizer with their forceful, skilful football. But the Romanians played a canny game and always looked electric on the break, passing with precision and moving intelligently off the ball. Thirteen minutes into the second half Hagi made it 3–1 to Romania with a stunning shot from the edge of the area, and that surely was that. But Argentina, roared on by Diego and the majority of the Rose Bowl crowd, desperately searched for a way back into the game. With fifteen minutes left they got it thanks to lethal Roma marksman Balbo.

That set up the proverbial 'grandstand finish', but Romania held out for a famous victory. The eastern Europeans' vibrant counter-attacking had surprised many but the Argentinians, despite the trauma surrounding their fallen idol, had won many friends with their exciting, creative play. For them it was the plane home with Diego, and for Romania the realization that this team could go all the way. Against Sweden in the quarter-finals, a cruel and perhaps unjustified penalty shoot-out defeat denied Romania a stab at Brazil in the semi-finals. But the memories of Anghel Iordanescu's team – Popescu, Hagi, Petrescu, Raducioiu, Dumitrescu et al – in full flow are some of the most enduring from an ultimately disappointing tournament.

66

West Ham 2   Munich 1860 0
European Cup Winners' Cup final
Wembley Stadium, attendance 100,000
19 May 1965

West Ham skipper Bobby Moore was to make a habit of walking up the thirty-nine steps to the royal box at Wembley in the mid-1960s. First up it was the FA Cup in 1964, and now the Cup Winners' Cup, played against a fine, similarly attack-minded German team. The big one was yet to come, but this one was big enough, only the second time an English club had won the trophy.

They hadn't found it easy to get through to the final, only managing to draw at home to Belgians La Gantoise in the first round and losing at Sparta Prague in the second, before edging past Lausanne in the quarter-final and Real Zaragoza in the semis. But they had hometown advantage in the final, and they played like it. Ron Greenwood's fluent-passing tactics were a joy to watch, with Martin Peters superb. 'In Europe you need more skill,' said Moore after the game, 'and Martin Peters added an extra quality to our game.' Another member of West Ham's team was a man who was to get to know Wembley pretty well a year later as a hat-trick scorer in the World Cup final.

Before the game, Hammers fans were worried about injuries to two key international attackers, outside-right Peter Brabrook and 'English Di Stefano' Johnny 'Budgie' Byrne. But young substitutes Alan Sealey and Brian Dear played like experienced Euro-pros, and Sealey scored both West Ham goals on sixty-nine and seventy-one minutes.

Wembley had rarely seen a better, more even-tempered game, and Moore said afterwards that it was the best game played by the last great West Ham team. His manager Ron Greenwood had something to add: 'This was Bobby Moore's greatest game. Technical perfection.' Actually the best was just round the corner in the same stadium, but this match certainly put him in the right sort of mood for winning trophies. The papers the next day carried pictures of Moore holding aloft the trophy on the shoulders of Hurst and Peters, the precursor to another famous picture to be taken in the not-too-distant future.

I was there . . . Ron Greenwood

It was a great chance for us to test ourselves at the top level, and we always fancied ourselves against continental opposition. Our side then was modelled on the continental game, and in many ways we were more suited to playing this kind of match than the cut and thrust of the English League. We played in the way I had always believed in, touch and go, a passing game, and we always looked to play it out from the back, of course, with Bobby Moore at the heart of the defence. He was a Colossus at this time.

The match was very even, the Germans were a very good side and played in the same way. But we got the goals at the right time and so we won it, which was fantastic, especially to do it at Wembley. And of course Bobby Moore, Geoff Hurst and Martin Peters were back again for the World Cup a few months later and this experience can only have helped, although they were such good players that in many ways this was meat and drink to them.

Afterwards the German captain Rudi Brunnemeier paid West Ham a great compliment when, the following season, he asked if he could spend a few days with us looking at our set-up and the way we trained, because he'd been so impressed with us.

The only sad thing about the match was that we'd prepared the football side so thoroughly that we hadn't organized anything for afterwards. There was no after-match dinner, there wasn't even any champagne. It was just a case of going back to Upton Park and getting in our cars. I remember Bobby Moore saying, 'We don't know how to celebrate at West Ham.'

67

Brighton 3 Sheffield Wednesday 2
League Division Three
Goldstone Ground, attendance 28,425
3 May 1977

eter Ward was the darling of the Brighton fans in
1976/7, and a quick burst of acceleration and a
lethal shot made him the most feared striker in the
division. Every time he got the ball he looked like
scoring, which he did thirty-six times that season. But
he nearly blew it for Brighton in this vital end-of-season
match.

Peter Taylor's team had just missed promotion the
season before. Alan Mullery took the reins and gave
the side a more ruthless edge. A win in this game would
be enough to take the Seagulls to the Second Division
for only the second time in their history. A huge crowd
packed the Goldstone terraces in anticipation of victory.

Ward was backed up by a gutsy team, with Ian 'Spider'
Mellor alongside him up front, Brian 'Nobby' Horton
running central midfield, and Irish international Peter
O'Sullivan on the flank. But Jack Charlton's Wednesday,
in seventh position, did their best to spoil the party on
the night, scoring in the first minute, and holding out
to go into the interval 1–0 up. Just after the restart
the nervous crowd could afford to relax slightly when

Brighton were awarded a penalty, and Ward stepped up to take it. Everyone was confident. He was deadly in the box . . . until he missed. But Ward made amends with a fifty-seventh-minute equalizer, and on seventy-one minutes he won another penalty for Brighton. A season's toil rested on one kick. Skipper Horton took it this time, and made no mistake. Local boy Steve Piper slammed home a third goal four minutes from time which meant that Wednesday's second goal, scored in the last minute, served only to add to the tension. The referee's final whistle signalled a celebratory crowd invasion, and Brighton were on a roll that eventually took them to the First Division and the FA Cup final.

68

Paris Saint Germain 4   Real Madrid 1
Uefa Cup quarter-final, second leg
Parc des Princes, attendance 45,000
21 April 1993

Hell hath no fury like a French football team denied a penalty, especially a penalty in the quarter-final of the Uefa Cup. Real Madrid beat Paris Saint Germain 3–1 in the first leg at the Bernabeu, an incredibly harsh result after a superb performance by the French. English referee David Elleray missed a blatant Sanchis foul on Ginola in the penalty area which might have made the game 2–2. And in the last minute Elleray adjudged French skipper Alain Roche had handled, sent him off, and gave Real a penalty which Michel converted. All this, you could say, made the second leg two weeks later rather keenly contested.

Back at the Parc des Princes PSG steamed into Real, making the breakthrough on thirty-three minutes through Liberian international George Weah with his sixth goal in the competition. But Real held out until, with just ten minutes left, David Ginola gleefully rammed the ball into the roof of the net from just outside the area to put PSG 2–0 up, and ahead on away goals. Suddenly it was the Spaniards' turn to pile forward in numbers. First they were denied a penalty, then sub

Alfonso missed a sitter from three yards out. But as they poured forward the Madrileños inevitably left gaps at the back, and Valdo scored a third for Paris on the counter. It was 3–0 on the night, 4–3 on aggregate, and the Parc des Princes was a sea of celebration.

But not for long. On the stroke of ninety minutes the game twisted yet again when Zamorano scored for the Spaniards to make it 3–1 and 4–4 on aggregate. Extra-time loomed. The crowd held their breath waiting for the Hungarian referee to blow, but he seemed to be waiting for someone to score and decide the whole thing. And on ninety-six minutes PSG obliged. Valdo curled in a free kick and Kambouaré headed home.

69

Argentina 0   Colombia 5
World Cup qualifying group A
River Plate Stadium, Buenos Aires, attendance 77,000
5 September 1993

The match that convinced the world that Colombia could win the 1994 World Cup. Never before had Argentina been so humiliated on their own soil. With Asprilla and Rincon playing like men possessed, Colombia ripped the Argentinian defences to shreds with a display of merciless finishing that left the massive Buenos Aires crowd stunned. Colombia had beaten Argentina 2–0 in Bogota, but to win 5–0 in Argentina was unthinkable. 'Verguenza!' (Shameful!) screamed Argentinian daily *El Grafico*, and this was one of the more restrained post-match headlines.

The Colombian side – built around Asprilla, Rincon, Valderrama and the erratic but brilliant Higuita – blended the traditional South American virtues of imagination, technique and close passing with hard work and discipline, and it seemed to work. After the Argentina match Colombian President Cesar Garcia awarded the entire team the Boyaca Cross, the highest medal a civilian can receive. The victory was part of a sequence of forty-one matches with only one defeat, and Pelé described the Colombians as the best side in South America. The world simply had to sit up and take notice, and bookies around the world slashed Colombia's USA 94 odds. Unfortunately everyone in Colombia wanted a piece of the action and in the end internal politics and outside pressures meant the team never lived up to its potential. The murder of defender Andreas Escobar and match-fixing allegations turned what could have been a glorious campaign into a tragic disaster.

70

England 3   Cameroon 2
(full-time score 2–2)
World Cup quarter-final
San Paolo Stadium, Naples, attendance 55,000
1 July 1990

ameroon, the side which had lit up Italia 90 with
their skill and power, did it again and almost sent
England's World Cup hopes up in smoke in this
dramatic quarter-final. If it hadn't been for the
Cameroon defenders losing their cool and Gary Lineker
keeping his, the Indomitable Lions would have lined up
against Germany in Turin rather than England. On a
sultry night in Naples Lineker's double penalty success
got England out of jail after their defence had been run
ragged all night by Oman Biyik and Roger Milla.

Coming into Italia 90, Cameroon had never been
beaten in any World Cup finals match, with three draws
in their first foray in 1982 and Argentina and Colombia
famously beaten in this competition. They were a team
of strange contrasts, on the one hand sublimely skilful
and superbly quick, on the other hand defensively
naive and to a certain extent brutal. This negative side
of the team's character strengthened England's position
as favourites as no fewer than four of Cameroon's first-
choice defenders were suspended for the quarter-final.
But with the sprightly thirty-eight-year-old Roger Milla

in their ranks, alongside players of the class of Oman Biyik and the dreadlocked Makanaky, Bobby Robson's men knew this match wouldn't be a walkover . . . and so it proved.

Even though Milla started on the bench, Cameroon began brightly and Shilton had to save smartly from Oman Biyik's header. But, with twenty-five minutes gone and somewhat against the run of play, David Platt scored his second crucial goal of the tournament and put England into the lead with a clinical downward header. The Africans could have wilted, but instead they came back stronger and England were lucky to hold on until half-time. After the break the shiny shaven head of Milla emerged from the tunnel, and from that moment England's problems really began.

The white shirts held on for the first fifteen minutes of the second half until Gascoigne brought down Milla. Penalty, 1–1. Four minutes later it was 2–1, Cameroon tearing England's sweeper system to shreds. Milla threaded a sublime pass through to Ekeke who lifted it neatly past Shilton. Robson immediately pulled off Butcher to give Trevor Steven a chance, and the five-man defence was abandoned. But England still looked decidedly second best and on their way out; Des Walker was hobbling and Mark Wright was suffering from a horrific head wound. Then, with eight minutes left, Lineker was upended by Massing just inside the box and England had a lifeline. Gary, England's hero, picked himself up and scored. Only in extra-time did England look like they could win the match, but it took yet another penalty. At the end of the first period Gascoigne threaded a perfect ball through to Lineker and this time it was the keeper N'Kono who brought him down. Penalty (again); Lineker (again); 3–2, and there was no way back for Cameroon.

England had won but Cameroon did the lap of honour. In their green, red and yellow they'd brightened the whole tournament and were unfortunate to be leaving now. England, however, sensed luck was on their side. But the next time penalties were to play such an important role, the ending was not to be such a happy one.

71

Charlton 6   Middlesbrough 6
League Division Two
The Valley, attendance 10,064
22 October 1960

The skies opened, the pitch turned into a patch of mud, the team kits became barely distinguishable, a certain young man named Brian Clough scored an away hat-trick and the 10,000 or so who'd turned up at the Valley saw a fantastic game of football.

The game swung one way then another at a phenomenal rate. Charlton took the lead only for Boro to score twice and make it 1–2. Then Charlton got two themselves to make it 3–2. 'Anything you can do we can do better' thought the Boro players, who duly went out and got another brace to go 3–4 up. Then Charlton equalized. Phew, what a game you might say. But this was just the first half. The weather wasn't doing a lot for the standard of football on offer, but boy was it creating a spectacle. In the second half Middlesbrough put their foot down to go 4–6 ahead, but Charlton pulled one back, and in the last minute Johnny Summers (who'd scored five in Charlton's 7–6 victory over Huddersfield two years before) equalized for the Addicks.

Only one other match has finished with the same scoreline, Leicester against Arsenal in 1930, and one man was particularly displeased about the fact: Brian Clough, who'd won his two England caps the previous year, apparently went bananas. As the story goes, he carried on complaining about the poor performance of his defenders so vigorously after the match that he was dumped off the coach in the middle of the night, many miles away from Middlesbrough, with the rain still lashing down.

72

Celtic 5   Partizan Belgrade 4
European Cup Winners' Cup, second leg
Parkhead, attendance 50,000
27 September 1989

An unbelievable night at Parkhead. Nine goals, more drama than a Shakespeare tragedy and, in the end, an unhappy ending for 50,000 hoarse-throated Celtic fans.

On a night when the emotions of the crowd soared and plummeted every time another goal rattled in, Celtic scored five – including four from Polish striker Dariusz Dziekanowski – but Partizan scored four, and those away goals ultimately cost the Glasgow side dear. Having lost 2–1 in Belgrade, Celtic opened the second leg in cavalier style. But errors get punished in European football and on this particular night some of Celtic's defied belief. After just seven minutes Pat Bonner scrambled away a shot, but from the corner Budimir Vijacic was left completely unmarked to head home. But Celtic hit back, and Walker and Coyne went close before Paul Elliott headed a Paul McStay free kick back across the area for Dziekanowski to head in.

Eighty seconds into the second half Celtic were level on aggregate after Dziekanowski fired home a shot that rebounded off the keeper. Now it was time for cool heads and patience but the fervour of the crowd drove Celtic forward and Partizan snatched another on the break. Now needing two to go through, Celtic powered into attack, and Dziekanowski scored yet again, volleying in a Roy Aitken cross, only for Partizan amazingly to get another. It was 3–3 on the night and still Celtic needed two. Incredibly they got them. First Walker turned in a low cross from Dziekanowski for the fourth and then, with Parkhead on the verge of mass hysteria, you know who did it again. It was 5–3 to Celtic and 6–5 on aggregate. They had done it. Or had they?

With the crowd whistling like their lives depended on it and ninety seconds left on the clock, Partizan launched the ball into the box. The Celtic defence hashed three opportunities to clear and Scepovic headed the Yugoslavs' fourth from six yards. Even more agonizing was the fact that Elliott was on the line to block the shot but Bonner's fingertips deflected the ball just beyond his head. The silence was thunderous and Celtic were out on away goals.

73

England 1   Belgium 0
(full-time score 0–0)
World Cup second round
Dall'Ara Stadium, Bologna, attendance 34,000
26 June 1990

England, through to the second round of Italia 90 thanks to a Mark Wright header against Egypt, could have wished for easier opponents than the fleet-footed Belgians, who netted six goals in the qualifying round to England's two. The Belgians included the captain Ceulemans, tall, agile goalkeeper Preud'homme, and their midfield genius Enzo Scifo.

In the opening minutes, Belgium looked like they'd walk it, passing the ball at pace and sauntering round the static England midfield seemingly at will. But eventually England pulled their game together, and a fascinating tactical match of (mainly Belgian) cat and (mainly English) mouse emerged. Ceulemans hit the base of a post in the first half, having run Wright ragged, Scifo in the second, having left his marker McMahon for dead. England, for their part, had a marvellous Barnes header – the culmination of an intricate five-man move – disallowed for an offside that never was.

Extra-time loomed, arrived, and seemed like finishing. Tired legs were not looking forward to penalties, but were unwilling to take risks. Then Gascoigne won a deep free kick with a minute to go. Some players would have played for time, passing the ball sideways or back towards the safety of the keeper. Not Gascoigne. He curled the ball into the box, where he'd spotted Platt in space. Facing the ball, Platt swivelled as it went over his shoulder, and volleyed past a startled Preud'homme, immediately ensuring himself a multi-million-pound future in Italian soccer. And to think he'd started the match on the bench. So famous was the finish, Platt now refers to it as 'that goal'.

You had to feel sorry for Belgium, but England, if only for that one moment of last-minute magic, deserved to shade it. A place in the quarter-finals against Cameroon, the team that was the life and soul of the Italia 90 party, was their reward.

74

Tottenham 2   Benfica 1
European Cup semi-final, second leg
White Hart Lane, attendance 60,000
5 April 1962

'The most electrifying ninety minutes of European
football I have ever seen on an English ground,'
wrote David Miller of the *Daily Express* after this
blood and thunder semi-final. Benfica, with a young
Eusebio in their side, had won the first leg 3–1, but
Spurs, who always preferred to bring their opponents
back to White Hart Lane for the second leg, knew what
they had to do. They had already overturned away defi-
cits against Gornik Zabbrze of Poland and the Czechs
of Dukla Prague en route to the semi and the massive
crowd fully expected the Spurs of Greaves and Blanchflower to do it again.

Guttman, Benfica's Hungarian coach, knew that the
atmosphere would be fierce and, fearful that his players
would be overawed, refused to let them warm up. And
they went straight out for the kick-off and straight into
the lead, Simores scoring after fifteen minutes. Spurs
were now 1–4 down on aggregate and so began a titanic
fightback. After thirty-eight minutes Smith made it 1–1
and five minutes into the second half a Blanchflower
penalty brought Spurs to within a goal of extra-time

with forty minutes still to play. From then on Tottenham laid siege to the Benfica goal. Three times they hit the woodwork in that second half, Dave Mackay smacking the bar in the last minute, but the ball just wouldn't go in.

'I lost count of the near misses,' said manager Bill Nicholson afterwards. Benfica went on to beat the great Real Madrid 5–3 in the final in Rome and Tottenham have never played in the European Cup since.

75

Liverpool 3 Borussia Mönchengladbach 1
European Cup final
Olympic Stadium, Rome, attendance 57,000
25 May 1977

It was only a matter of time before Liverpool, the irresistible force of English football, won the European Cup, and on 25 May 1977 they did it in style. With the Kop transported lock, stock and barrel to the Olympic Stadium in Rome and with Kevin Keegan in sparkling form in his farewell game before joining Hamburg, the Reds powered past German champions Borussia Mönchengladbach to lift the trophy for the first time ever. Goals from McDermott, Smith and a penalty from Neal sealed a famous victory. The biggest surprise of the night was not how well they played, but that Tommy Smith scored with his head.

Liverpool played some sublime football, and were leading comfortably through McDermott's goal when little Danish international Alan Simonsen equalized for Borussia early in the second half. This was the Germans' best spell of the match and Clemence was called into action several times to keep the English champions in the game. And with Borussia unable to get past Clemence, Liverpool scored from the most unlikely of sources: Steve Heighway fired in a corner and, charging in at the near post, left-back Tommy Smith thundered a header beyond the keeper. Now it was Liverpool's turn to go on the attack, rampantly surging at the Borussia defence. In the eighty-third minute, Keegan was chopped down by Berti Vogts and Neal stepped up to fire the Reds into a 3–1 lead from the spot.

Bob Paisley's men had done it, just four days after losing the FA Cup final to Manchester United, and Rome was painted red and white. The celebrations lasted all through the night; supporters even discovered the team's hideaway and joyously threw several Liverpool players into the swimming pool. It was the first of many similar European celebrations over the next eight years.

I was there . . . Emlyn Hughes

As soon as we'd beaten St Etienne in the quarter-final we knew we would win the European Cup. We murdered Zurich in the semi-final and I honestly don't think there's a single person in that team who thought we'd lose to Borussia. But the match still had to be won.

It sounds corny but when I went up to pick up the trophy I wasn't thinking about this team, the Kevin Keegans and the Steve Heighways, I was thinking about the Ian St Johns and the Roger Hunts, the players from previous Liverpool teams who'd taught us how to win in Europe. They'd shown us the way. We hadn't won the European Cup, Liverpool Football Club had won it.

We knew we were a good side. We never had team talks under Bill Shankly or Bob Paisley, the only thing we talked about was the other team's free kicks and corners. We never thought about the opposition because we knew that if we went out and produced what we were capable of then we would win, whoever we were playing.

What I do remember about that night in Rome is the fans, they were fantastic. It was like walking out for a home game. And after the match we went back to the hotel and they laid on this banquet for us. There was lobster and crab, ham, beef, everything. It was an enormous spread. But after you've played you're never really hungry and so even after we'd eaten, and the directors and the wives and everyone had eaten, there was still plenty left. So I went up to the chairman, John Smith, and said, 'Mr Smith, why not let some of the fans in to finish off this food, it would be a great PR move for the club.' So he said all right. There were some fans outside and they'd been singing and cheering, so they opened the door to let them in. But there was about 2,000 of them out there, and they charged in. As soon as they saw the spread they went for the food, it was like a plague of locusts, like they hadn't eaten for days. They weren't the slightest bit interested in us.

76

Watford 7   Southampton 1
(full-time score, 5–5 on aggregate)
League Cup second round, second leg
Vicarage Road, attendance 15,992
2 September 1980

First Division leaders Southampton, Keegan et al, had drubbed Second Division Watford 4–0 at the Dell and were expecting to cruise the second leg, so they rested their former European Player of the Year. Oops.

Watford went into the interval 2–0 up, with goals from Poskett and Train. By seventy-five minutes Patching and Bolton had doubled Watford's score but, disastrously, a Steve Sims own goal looked to have tipped the aggregate balance in Southampton's favour. Then, with four minutes to go, Jenkins crashed home for the Hornets to put the game into extra-time. In the extra half-hour seventeen-year-old substitute Nigel Callaghan scored a sixth for Watford with his first touch of the ball, and Malcolm Poskett wrapped things up five minutes from the end. Graham Taylor's team had humiliated the League leaders, and made a name for themselves that wasn't going to be forgotten in a hurry.

Chief Executive Eddie Plumley said after the match: 'With fifteen minutes to go we opened the exit gates as usual, but there were more people coming in than going out!' It wasn't the end of Watford's League Cup exploits, and the Vicarage Road turnstiles continued to click furiously that season. In the third round they drew European champions Nottingham Forest at home, and thrashed them 4–1. Eventually they were knocked out in the quarter-final by Coventry.

77

Colchester 3   Leeds United 2
FA Cup fifth round
Layer Road, Colchester, attendance 16,000
13 February 1971

his was the great Leeds side, the one that anyone over thirty-five can reel off from memory, even now: Reaney, Charlton, Hunter, Giles, Clarke . . . managed by Don Revie, they were chasing a League, Cup and Uefa Cup treble.

And this was the great Colchester side, the one that, against all the odds, got to the sixth round of the FA Cup, even though they were only in the Fourth Division. Colchester's secret weapon was Ray Crawford, twice an England international, who'd been Ipswich Town's top scorer in their First Division Championship season. But that was ten years before. Crawford was one of six players over thirty in the Colchester side, which led to their inevitable nickname 'Grandad's Army'.

Remarkably, Crawford re-found his former touch in the first half as Colchester's attacking football worried Leeds. On eighteen minutes he headed past Gary Sprake, and before half-time he doubled the score while lying on the ground after a collision with the Leeds keeper, his eighth goal of Colchester's Cup campaign. Whatever Revie said at half-time, it didn't do the trick, and ten

241

minutes after the restart Dave Simmons headed a third for Colchester. The Fourth Division legs began to tire as the match progressed, and Leeds began to dominate. But having pulled two goals back, through Norman Hunter and Johnny Giles, they just couldn't get the vital third, mainly due to some inspired goalkeeping from Graham Smith. Grandad's Army lived to fight another day, at Everton, in fact, in the quarter-finals, where they lost 5–0.

Colchester's manager Dick Graham said before the match that if his team won he would scale the walls of Colchester Castle. He was as good as his word, but the Essex side has never reached such dizzy heights again.

I wasn't there . . . Billy Bremner

It's my claim to fame that I was injured for the Colchester match. I was at home watching *Grandstand* and after about twenty-five minutes Frank Bough came on with this huge grin on his face and I thought, 'Oh, oh, we're in trouble here.' Sure enough, we were 1–0 down. Still, I knew the boys would be OK. Then he came on again with an even bigger grin and I thought, 'Oh no, not another', and it was 2–0. Then he came on with the biggest grin you've ever seen in your life and I thought, 'Oh no, we're really in stook'; it was 3–0.

I was getting worried so I switched the TV off and put the radio on. Then we pulled it back to 3–1, and then it was 3–2. 'Ah no problem,' I thought, 'the boys'll pull it back.' So I switched the radio off and put the TV back on. When it was time for the results I think Frank

Bough was doing somersaults and I thought, 'Oh no, why did I switch the radio off?'

That night I met Big Jack in the pub and he told me it was just one of those days. He said the last fifteen minutes had been like the Alamo but we were never going to score. But that match typifies what is great about the FA Cup. Whenever anyone looks at changing the game, especially the FA Cup like in Spain where all the teams are seeded, just get them to look at this match. It's what the FA Cup is all about.

78

St Mirren 0   Celtic 5
Scottish Premier Division
Love Street
3 May 1985

his wasn't so much one match as two. If Celtic were
to win the League, not only did they have to beat
St Mirren by three clear goals, they also had to pray
that championship rivals Hearts would lose at Dundee.

Celtic got the three goals they needed within thirty-
two minutes thanks to one from Brian McClair and two
from Maurice Johnstone, but Hearts were still level with
Dundee. Eight minutes into the second half Celtic were
cruising at 5–0 up but their fans weren't watching any
more, they were listening to their trannies. With ten
minutes to go and with the ball safely nestled in the St
Mirren keeper's hands, the massed ranks of Celtic fans
behind him suddenly, surreally, erupted: Hearts were
1–0 down thanks to a goal from Dundee substitute
Albert Kidd. (The terraces even erupted at Ibrox where
the Rangers fans, on hearing that Kidd had scored,
assumed it was Walter Kidd, the Hearts captain.) Back
at Love Street there were songs of celebration on the
terraces once Kidd scored a second for Dundee. Celtic
secured their thirty-fourth championship.

It was an incredible climax to a remarkable title race.

While Hearts, in control for most of the season, could only blame themselves, due credit went to Celtic who'd won their last eight matches on the trot and were undefeated in their last sixteen games.

If Hearts' hearts were broken then they were to be completely shattered a week later when they lost 3–0 to Aberdeen in the Scottish Cup final to turn their Double plans into a Double disaster.

79

Manchester United 4   Blackpool 2
FA Cup final
Wembley Stadium, attendance 99,000
24 April 1948

If ever a match was sure to produce a glut of goals, this was it. The great Blackpool side, boasting the likes of Stan Mortensen and Stanley Matthews, scored eighteen goals in their run-in to the final, conceding only one. United, on the other hand, managed by Matt Busby, played with the 'famous five' in the front line – Delaney, Morris, Rowley, Pearson and Mitten – and themselves had scored eighteen in their six matches, all against First Division opposition, all away from home. Everybody expected a corker, and by God they got one.

Blackpool opened the scoring with a penalty by Shimwell after the speedy Mortensen had been brought down just outside the box by Chilton. 'Electric heels' Mortensen helped himself to Blackpool's second, five minutes after United's Rowley made the most of a Black-pool defensive blunder to dribble an equalizer into an empty net. United managed to cut off the supply line to Matthews in the second half and started to dominate. But they were still trailing with twenty-one minutes remaining, until Rowley dived spectacularly to head in the United equalizer. It was 2–2 and anyone's game:

Mortensen hit a netbuster, but Crompton saved mag-nificently and, Schmeichel-like, threw it quickly out to Anderson. His pass went via Pearson to Lorimer, who fired United into the lead. The fourth goal, ballooning in off a defender from an Anderson shot, only served to distort the result of a classic Cup final.

80

Leicester City 3 Leatherhead 2
FA Cup fourth round
Filbert Street, attendance 32,090
25 January 1975

Chris Kelly, the non-League striker who became known as the 'Leatherhead lip', confidently predicted on *Football Focus* that Leatherhead would 'go all the way to Wembley'. Funnily enough it didn't happen, but they very nearly got one step closer at the expense of First Division Leicester City.

Kelly himself put Leatherhead 2–0 up at Filbert Street, cheered on not only by Surrey fans but also by a fair few Nottingham Forest supporters whose match at the City Ground had been called off due to a frozen pitch. Playing in a fetching all-green strip, Leatherhead stunned the chilly Leicester crowd with their first-half performance. They had made it to the prestigious third round by beating Colchester, and saw off Brighton 1–0 at the Goldstone Ground. Was another shock on the cards? No. The Foxes did eventually warm to the task and, after drawing level, made it safely through to the fifth round. Frank Worthington chipped in a free kick which was destined for the top corner until the Leatherhead keeper got a hand to it, but Steve Earle was there to hammer in the rebound.

1975 was the year of the underdog in the FA Cup. Wimbledon beat Burnley at Turf Moor, the first non-League side since 1945 to beat a First Division team on their own ground, then stunned Leeds by drawing at Elland Road and forcing a replay (only losing when a Johnnie Giles shot deflected off Harry Bassett's backside) and Altrincham drew 1–1 with Everton at Goodison Park. If Second Division Fulham had beaten West Ham in the final no one would have batted an eyelid.

81

England 3   Poland 0
World Cup group five
Universitario Stadium, Monterrey, Mexico,
attendance 22,700
11 June 1986

A disappointing defeat against Portugal, a frustrating goalless draw with Morocco: it looked like England would be out of Mexico 86 before the fun had hardly started. There were no two ways about it. They had to beat Poland, an old World Cup enemy, to make sure of qualifying for the next round.

Injuries, suspensions and bad form forced England manager Bobby Robson's tactical hand; out went skipper Bryan Robson, Ray Wilkins, Chris Waddle and Mark Hateley, and in came Steve Hodge, Trevor Steven, Peter Reid and Peter Beardsley. In the early stages Fenwick's cumbersome marking gave Boniek a chance, but the Juventus man was unusually profligate. After that scare the game went England's way. Suddenly Robson's men were all speed and purpose, a completely different proposition from the lacklustre, lumbering side of the earlier matches.

After just eight minutes England scored their first goal of the tournament: Trevor Steven's cross found cast-armed Gary Lineker who joyously swept the ball home.

Then on fourteen minutes the number ten half-volleyed a second past Polish keeper Mlynarczyk after a neat Beardsley–Hodge combination. Ten minutes before the interval he completed his hat-trick after the keeper fumbled Steven's corner. It went straight through his hands, a far cry from Tomaszewski in 1973. Gary Lineker, in thirty-five short minutes, had become the golden boy of English football, a title he was to cherish for six more years.

England took their foot off the accelerator in the second half, with Butcher and Fenwick carrying injuries, but nobody was complaining. Suddenly the country had a team that looked capable of winning the World Cup – well, maybe – and in Beardsley and Lineker a strikeforce that looked capable of unlocking the tightest of defences.

82

Tottenham 2 Sheffield United 2
FA Cup final
Crystal Palace, attendance 114,815
20 April 1901

Since the year ended in a one, Tottenham had a chance. In fact it turned out to be a historic year as Spurs became the first and only non-League club (they were then part of the Southern League) to win the FA Cup.

The match was hailed as proof that the softy southerners were beginning to get their act together, and Spurs were also the first truly London-based team to lift the trophy. With Crystal Palace at bursting point, there were 114,815 in the ground to be exact, the third largest Cup final crowd ever witnessed a game of drama and outrageous controversy. After going a goal down Spurs had fought back to lead 2–1 when United's Bert Lipsham hit a rasping shot from the edge of the box. Spurs keeper Clawley couldn't hold it and as the ball broke free defender William Bennett booted it out. United appealed for a corner, Spurs for a goal kick. The linesman duly indicated a corner but the referee inexplicably gave a goal. After that the players were too astonished to finish the game properly and it took a replay a week later for Spurs to clinch the Cup.

TOTTENHAM 2   SHEFFIELD UNITED 2

After the match Tottenham officials tied ribbons in the team's colours to the handles of the Cup, so starting a tradition that has continued ever since.

83

Hereford 2   Newcastle United 1
(full-time score 1–1)
FA Cup third round replay
Edgar Street, attendance 15,000
5 February 1972

Newcastle United came away from this Edgar Street fixture covered from head to toe in winter mud. But it was the egg on their faces that made them look really daft. Even though the Southern League outfit had managed a 2–2 draw with the north-eastern giants in early January, a mutton-chopped Malcolm Mac-Donald had been bragging that he'd score five in the replay. He had plenty of time to brag: the match was postponed four times and a month had passed since the first game.

More than 15,000 fans packed into the compact Edgar Street ground to see Newcastle dominate the early stages, but keeper Fred Potter kept MacDonald and co. at bay with several fine saves. When MacDonald did score for Newcastle, against the run of play, there were seven minutes left and it all looked over. Then Radford and George stepped in, and their Arsenal namesakes couldn't have affected a more significant turnaround.

With six minutes remaining Radford dug the ball out of a puddle, pushed it several yards forward into another one, and hit a screaming thirty-yard shot past the bewildered Liam McFaul. In extra-time, when the police had cleared the snorkel parkas off the pitch, Radford put substitute Ricky George through to cap a remarkable performance with a hugely applauded goal. He's still being bought drinks down Hereford way. This was the first time a non-League team had beaten First Division opposition for twenty-three years, and still makes Newcastle fans wince when the goals are replayed every year on *Football Focus* in early January.

Just four days later Edgar Street was host to another top-flight team in the fourth round. This time it was West Ham, who scrambled their way to a 0–0 draw before putting the plucky Bulls out 3–1 in an Upton Park replay. Hereford were elected to the Football League at the end of the season, but they'd already played their way into FA Cup legend.

84

Liverpool 7   Tottenham 0
League Division One
Anfield, attendance 50,705
2 September 1978

A couple of weeks into Ossie Ardiles and Ricky Villa's first season in English football with Tottenham, Liverpool decided to give them a welcoming present at Anfield. It finished 7–0 and the Argentinian duo were not available for comment after the game: or was it just that they were dumbstruck?

Keith Burkinshaw had stunned the world with the double signing just weeks after Ardiles had inspired Argentina to victory in the World Cup. In Buenos Aires to complete the Ardiles deal, the little midfielder had asked his new boss, almost as an afterthought, if he liked Ricky Villa because he would come as well. Burkinshaw couldn't believe his luck. The *Guardian* reported: 'It was as if the janitor had gone to buy a tin of paint and come back with a Velázquez.'

After this match the Argentinian duo must have been wondering if they'd made the right decision. Dalglish, Kennedy, Johnson (two), Neal and McDermott scored the goals which sent Tottenham into seventh hell. The last goal was the best, starting with Clemence in the Liverpool goal and, via half the Liverpool team, ending up in the back of the Spurs net before you could blink. Afterwards Reds manager Bob Paisley described it as 'one of the best goals in the history of the club'.

85

Tout Puissant Englebert (Zaire) 1
Asante Kotoko (Ghana) 2
African Champions Cup final, second leg
20th May Stadium, Kinshasa
10 January 1971

More than 75,000 people crammed inside the 20th May Stadium in Zaire (built to accommodate just 45,000) for this second-leg match between the two greatest African club sides at the time. But this match really was more than a game. Having already won the Champions Cup twice, if Tout Puissant Englebert (TP) beat Asante Kotoko to make it a third victory they would keep the trophy and the new one, as is traditional in Africa, would be named after Zaire president Mobutu Sesse-Seko.

After a 1–1 draw two weeks earlier in the first leg in Ghana, the president arrived at the ground fully expecting this great honour and the great political prestige that would come with it. TP took the lead, the crowd went mad and the president smiled. But with nothing to lose the Ghanaian team flooded forward and pulled it back to 1–1. Now playing with confidence and panache, and sensing TP's nervousness, Asante Kotoko did the unthinkable – they took the lead. It stayed 2–1, and Sesse-Seko didn't stick

around to see the trophy presentation. He left the
ground in an angry rage and TP haven't won the Cup
since.

86

Ireland 1   Italy 0
World Cup qualifying round, group E
Giants Stadium, New York, attendance 73,000
18 June 1994

This was one of the most eagerly awaited matches of
the tournament. New York was the setting, and the
Giants Stadium was a sea of green, full of both ex-
pat Paddies and thousands of travelling Irish fans, many
of whom freely admitted they'd sold their grandmothers
to get there.

It was hellishly hot but Ireland rattled the Italians
from the beginning of the game, pressing hard in typical
Jack Charlton style, and never allowing them to settle.
Then, out of the blue the ball fell to Houghton, who
cracked a dipper over the out-of-position Pagliuca and
into the net. Whether he meant to place the ball so
expertly or not hardly mattered, you could hear the
celebratory roar from New York in Dublin, and the roar
from Dublin in Rome. The Italians never really
threatened an equalizer. This Italy performance was
typical of Sacchi's side, who got to the final despite
showing only flashes of form.

Ireland's World Cup faltered thereafter: they lost to
Mexico, drew 0–0 with Norway and were put out of the
tournament 2–0 by a vastly superior Holland side. 'At

a tournament notable for its quality, Ireland stood out as beggars at the banquet,' said Eamonn Dunphy afterwards. In a way Jack's dream ended here, not a year and a half later at Anfield.

87

Manchester United 2   Barcelona 1
European Cup Winners' Cup final
Rotterdam, attendance 45,000
15 May 1991

Revenge is sweet, they say, but it's rarely come sweeter in football than for 1991 Player of the Year Mark Hughes, released by Barcelona two years previously and back to haunt them with a typical display of bullish centre-forwardry.

This season saw the English clubs' return to European competition after Heysel, and United battled their way to this Cup Winners' Cup final with as much determination as skill. More than 30,000 United fans travelled to Rotterdam, and they roared as Hughes tapped in a Bruce header to put United ahead on sixty-eight minutes. But such an easy goal was not good enough for Hughes, who sportingly awarded it to Bruce. No, Hughes wanted a corker to get his own back on his former employers and, rounding the young Barça keeper Busquets and finding himself with the narrowest of angles to shoot from, he thwacked the ball home with all the venom he could muster.

Ronald Koeman made the 30,000 chew their nails with a free kick that confounded the laws of physics with ten minutes to go, and Barcelona might have snatched a late equalizer, but that would have been unfair: to Alex Ferguson, who became the second man to win the Cup with two different clubs (United and Aberdeen), to United and, above all, to Mark 'Sparky' Hughes.

88

Wimbledon 1   Liverpool 0
FA Cup final
Wembley Stadium, attendance 98,203
15 May 1988

'The day Wimbledon lost its virginity'. That's how
Sam Hammam described the greatest day in the
history of football in SW19. A footballing classic it
might not have been, but for sheer David v. Goliath
drama and nail-biting tension it was the sort of match
only the FA Cup final can serve up.

Remembered best for Dave Beasant's penalty save,
the first-ever in an FA Cup final, this was eleven bargain-
basement battlers defying the odds to beat by far and
away the best team in the land. No one had given them
a hope. Liverpool – Barnes, Beardsley, Hansen et al –
had swept away all before them all season until they
bumped into Bobby Gould's Krazy Gang in the
Wembley tunnel. With Vinny psyched up, aided by a
quick bout of banging his head on the tunnel wall, and
Dennis Wise switched to the left to stifle John Barnes,
the Dons, who'd been down the pub the night before,
battled their way to one of the most unexpected Cup
final victories in the history of the competition.

In the glorious May sunshine Wimbledon, with a
tactical masterplan drawn up by coach Don Howe,

hustled Liverpool out of their stride, snatched a goal from a set-piece and held on heroically. 'The crazy gang have beaten the culture club,' pontificated an over-excited John Motson as the final whistle sounded. The match hinged on an incident in the thirty-fifth minute. Latching on to a through-ball Beardsley wriggled past the illegal challenge of Andy Thorn to race clear and poke the ball past Beasant, only for referee Brian Hill to pull him back for a Liverpool free kick. Dalglish, who stood throughout the entire match, was outraged, and a minute later Lawrie Sanchez put Wimbledon 1–0 up. When Beasant saved from Aldridge's spot kick in the second half, the blue and yellow ribbons were already being tied on to the Cup. 'The players knew they'd win,' said Wimbledon manager Bobby Gould, 'they had an inner belief.'

I was there . . . Dave Beasant

When we got to the Wembley dressing-room Bobby Gould had put all these cuttings on the wall, all the papers saying we were going to lose, just to wind us up. We just wanted to get out on the pitch, although there was a lot of time spent in the toilets. Even in the warm-up I didn't want the ball to go past me, I wouldn't let anyone put it in the net. I warmed up with Alan Cork and I wouldn't let him score.

When Beardsley was clean through I had heard the referee's whistle but I still didn't want to get beaten; I was playing for real when I tried to stop his shot, but when it went in I knew it wasn't a goal.

We had eighteen penalties against us that season and I only saved three, but at least I stopped the most important one. Then they had a corner straight after the penalty and it came right to me. It was an easy catch, and I dropped it! But we held on, the whistle went, and we'd done it. After the match the Liverpool players rushed off – I can't think why – but Bruce Grobbelaar made a point of shaking my hand and he gave me these glasses with tennis racket lenses he'd had made and we swapped shirts. None of the other players could because by the time we got back to the dressing-rooms they'd gone!

I got the match ball as well for being the winning captain, and you should have heard Sanchez wingeing on to Bobby about it, saying, 'I should have it, I scored the goal.' In fact I don't think he's ever forgiven me for it.

89

Leeds 4   Stuttgart 1
European Cup first round, second leg
Elland Road, attendance 20,457
30 September 1992

Stuttgart could have been excused for feeling a little complacent having won the first leg of this European Cup first rounder 3–0 in Germany, but at least they scraped the result they needed on the night. Or so they thought.

A flowing-locked Gary Speed gave Leeds a morale-boosting early lead, but the Germans soon equalized when Andreas Buck scored a vital away goal. Gary McAllister converted a penalty to give the huge Elland Road crowd a little hope at the half-time break.

In the second half there was wave after wave of awesome Leeds pressure as they strove to get the three goals they needed to get into the second round. Eric Cantona and Lee Chapman (who'd given Buchwald the runaround all match) netted second-half goals, but in the last ten minutes Leeds just couldn't find the killer touch to finish things off. At the end of the game the Stuttgart players fell flat on their backs, having been subjected to ninety minutes of British football at its best. They were knackered, but they thought they had won – or at least lost narrowly enough to have ensured qualification. They were wrong, oh how they were wrong. Four foreigners had finished the match on the pitch for Stuttgart and the rules stipulated a maximum of three, so Uefa ordered a rematch in Barcelona. There could only be one result this time, and Carl Shutt duly put Leeds through to the next round, 'The Battle of Britain' v. Rangers.

90

Scotland 2   Wales 0
World Cup qualifying play-off
Anfield, attendance 50,800
12 October 1977

With the Kop packed full of Scots wearing tammies,
Scotland booked their place in the World Cup
in Argentina by dumping Wales out of the
competition in a highly charged and highly controversial
night at Anfield. Wales knew that a draw would keep
their hopes alive but their chances were dashed when
the Welsh FA switched the match to Anfield because of
crowd restrictions at Ninian Park. Most of the tickets
fell into Scottish hands, and Anfield was like a mini-
Hampden when the teams emerged.

Ally MacLeod's Scotland started the better of the two
sides, forcing a couple of corners and screaming for a
penalty when Dalglish appeared to be brought down in
the box by Dai Davies. But as the game settled Wales
began to create chances of their own. Mainly composed
of players from the English lower divisions, Wales played
the better football in the intense atmosphere. Peter Sayer
went close and John Toshack hit the bar in front of his
beloved Kop.

Then the crucial incident. With the scores deadlocked
the ball was hoisted into the Welsh box and Scotland

were suddenly awarded a penalty for handball. Handball it indeed was, but it was Scotland striker Joe Jordan who was the offender not poor David Jones. Masson scored and Wales were out of the World Cup. Dalglish got another in the last minute and the Scots were heading for Argentina. Or was it Brazil? One geographically challenged Scottish newspaper proclaimed the next day, 'We're on our way to Rio'.

91

Norwich 1   Bayern Munich 1
Uefa Cup second round, second leg
Carrow Road, attendance 20,829
3 November 1993

This was the night Norwich stuffed one hundred years of tractor jokes down the throats of rival fans everywhere. The men in the canary yellow shirts (the ones with the birdshit speckles) went to the Olympic Stadium and humbled the mighty Bayern Munich. The officials of the great German club didn't even know where Norwich was when the draw was made, but Mike Walker's team was about to put Norfolk on the footballing map of Europe.

It was surreal, Norwich 2–0 up at the home of thrice European Cup-winners Bayern. Jeremy Goss's spectacular thirteenth-minute volley and then Mark Bowen's goal on the half-hour stunned the Munich crowd and just about everyone else too. 'I just thought, "Cor blimey what's this?" ' recalls then Canaries boss Mike Walker. 'Before the match I thought we'd do well to get a draw because we were going into the unknown, although having said that I was always confident that the way we played would help us in European competition. And on the night we played five at the back, we passed the ball well, we got a couple of breaks and took our goals brilliantly.' When Nerlinger scored to make it 2–1 it looked like normal service was about to be resumed but Norwich held on, riding their luck at times, leaving Bayern everything to do in the return match in frosty Norfolk.

Two weeks later, with an atmosphere Carrow Road had never seen before, Norwich gave it everything they had and it was enough . . . just. Valencia's goal for Bayern made it tenser than Christmas Eve in a turkey hutch, but Jeremy Goss did it again and Norwich went through to meet Inter Milan.

92

Brighton 2   Manchester United 2
(full-time score 2–2)
FA Cup final
Wembley Stadium, attendance 100,000
21 May 1983

lthough Manchester United went on to win the
replay, this will be remembered as Brighton's final.
The south coast side played a stirring part in this
draw, even though they were without their suspended
skipper Steve Foster and, but for a last-seconds-of-extra-
time save from Gary Bailey, could easily have lifted the
trophy. This Cup final caught the imagination more than
most, with the overwhelming underdogs (freshly rel-
egated to the Second Division under the charismatic
caretaker-managership of white-shoed Jimmy Melia)
fighting against the traditional might of United.

Bailey's save is usually credited as a miss by Gordon
Smith, who will always be remembered for his error (not
least by the Brighton fanzine *And Smith Must Score*). 'I
wasn't expecting a pass from Robbo. Robbo never
passes,' was Smith's post-match explanation, referring to
his team-mate, the Irish international Mick Robinson's
part in the move. In Smith's favour his weak shot came
from tired legs after 120 minutes of energy-draining
football. And, as most people forget, he did score
Brighton's first goal, a far-post header on fourteen

minutes that put them into the lead. Brighton full-back Chris Ramsey, temporarily crippled after a Whiteside foul, was unable to challenge when 'Big Norm' headed on a Duxbury cross. Stapleton headed an equalizer for United and the match looked over when a brilliant Muhren pass set up Ray Wilkins who, in remarkably uncrab-like fashion, curled his shot into Mosely's net on seventy-two minutes. But Brighton showed the spirit that had got them to the final, and refused to give up. With three minutes remaining, Gary Stevens walloped a Jimmy Case corner into the net to send the game into extra-time. Smith will never be able to forget what followed, and United, despite Foster's return, comfortably won the replay 4–0.

93

Guiseley 4   Gresley Rovers 4
(full-time score 3–3)
FA Vase final
Wembley Stadium, attendance 11,314
4 May 1991

They don't come much more exciting than this. Guiseley, home of Harry Ramsden's famous biggest-ever chip shop, go three up against Gresley within thirty minutes in front of 11,000 fans at the home of football. Guiseley had already won the Northern Counties League title and it looked like the Double was in the bag. But just before half-time Guiseley pulled a goal back, and midway through the second half they made it 3–2. With the clock ticking away, though, Guiseley were getting ready to celebrate when Gresley's Keiron Smith, from twenty yards, launched himself into, er, FA Vase folklore with the equalizer. What a comeback, what a final, but it wasn't over yet.

In extra-time Gresley did it yet again, going 4–3 up and sending their fans into delirium. It looked like the men from Guiseley had been well and truly battered, until Alan Roberts came along. With two minutes left Roberts stretched for a cross, and the ball ricocheted over the Gresley keeper's head for 4–4. Unbelievable. Guiseley club secretary Phil Rogerson recalls: 'He just stuck out a foot and it looped over the keeper, although he insisted afterwards that it was a memorable free kick.'

It was an astonishing match, but after poor Gresley's superhuman comeback they lost the replay 3–1 the following week at Sheffield United's Bramall Lane.

94

The best Oxford United side in the history of the club took time off their tense relegation struggle to give favourites QPR an unexpected mauling at Wembley, to become the last winners of the Milk Cup.

Trevor Hebberd masterminded Oxford's greatest-ever result from midfield, assisted by Les Phillips and a twenty-four-year-old Irish Glaswegian by the name of Ray Houghton. Hebberd scored the first on forty minutes and had a foot in the other two, playing a neat one-two with Houghton on fifty-one and putting Aldridge through with four minutes left. His shot was saved, but Charles netted the rebound to cap a famous victory. Rangers, who'd lifted the trophy when it was known simply as the League Cup back in 1967, didn't know what had hit them, especially manager Jim 'Bald Eagle' Smith who was left questioning a recent career move. He'd left Oxford, after taking them from the Third to the First Division in successive years, to take the reins at Rangers.

It wasn't Oxford's only triumph that season either. They eventually finished eighteenth in the First Division and maintained top-flight status for another year, eventually dropping out of the big time in 1988, never to return. Wembley must seem a long way off now.

Scotland 1   Italy 0
World Cup qualifying group eight
Hampden Park, attendance 100,393
9 November 1965

On a night of fierce passion and euphoria at Hampden
Park, Scotland earned the victory that meant the
Tartan Army's planned World Cup invasion of
England was still on. The Scots had two games left, both
against Italy. Two wins would mean definite qualification, a win and a draw would mean a play-off place,
so on the night of the home tie Hampden Park heaved
with 100,000 expectant fans.

Jock Stein made a couple of bold decisions in his team
selection, dropping Denis Law and recalling Jim Baxter
who'd broken his leg a year earlier. Only five players
from the side which had lost to Poland in the previous
match played. The Italian team was packed with stars
from the AC Milan and Inter teams which had won
the European Cup the previous three years, including
Facchetti, Mazzola and Rivera. But it was no surprise
that they were immediately on the defensive as the match
got under way. Scotland threw everything into attack
with 'Slim' Jim Baxter at the heart of everything, but
the experienced Italians soaked it all up. And, to the
crowd's frustration, that was the pattern of the match,

although the Italians had their moments on the break with Mazzola and Riva both going close.

As the disappointed Scots fans began to drift away, their team mounted one last attack on the fortress that was the Italian defence. Baxter picked up the ball and for once split the Italian defence for the advancing John Greig to crash the ball inside Negri's near post. The crowd went mad and at the end refused to disperse until the players had done a lap of honour. But in the end it was all to no avail as a month later Stein's injury-ravaged side lost 3–0 in Naples . . . and the Scots missed the party.

96

Everton 3   Bayern Munich 1
European Cup Winners' Cup semi-final,
second leg
Goodison Park, attendance 49,476
24 April 1985

I n the best Toffee era since the days of Dixie Dean, Everton – managed by Howard Kendall and including the likes of Sheedy, Reid, Gray, Ratcliffe, Mountfield and Sharp – were on a trophy roll. They'd won the FA Cup the year before, now they were after a unique European Cup Winners' Cup and League Double. Having rollercoastered their way to the semis (after a stuttery 1–0 first-round win over the University of Dublin!) they battled to a hard-earned draw in Munich to set up this thunderous semi-final second leg.

The Germans, with their fine European pedigree (including three European Cup wins in the seventies), looked like a tough proposition. However, on the night Bayern simply didn't know what hit them. It was Graeme Sharp, Andy Gray and Trevor Steven, in fact, on the end of three of a bucketful of sweetly worked blue moves on a memorable night that put Everton through to the final against Rapid Vienna in Rotterdam. Gray, Sheedy and Steven brought Everton their one and only European trophy in the last match of a memorable season in which they also won the First Division title, completely to overshadow neighbours Liverpool who ended the campaign empty-handed. In the year of Heysel it was to be the last British success in Europe until 1991.

97

Newcastle 1   Brighton 3
League Division Two
St James's Park, attendance 28,425
6 May 1979

here were three sets of fans in the huge St James's Park crowd: Brighton fans, cheering on their heroes who would go up to the First Division for the first time in their history if they won; Newcastle fans (a few of them cheering on Brighton because if the Seagulls went up rivals Sunderland would stay down); and Sunderland fans, cheering on Newcastle for the first and last time in their lives, hoping their neighbours and bitter rivals would do them a favour. Brighton had just missed out on promotion the year before when a stale draw between Southampton and Tottenham, in which Steve Williams missed a penalty, had meant that both sides went up when any other result would have seen Brighton promoted.

But this was a classic side, with Brian 'Nobby' Horton running the midfield, Mark Lawrenson splendid at the back and Peter Ward still a force to be reckoned with up front. The previous season's disappointment hadn't blunted their form. Brighton were superb on the day, too, going into the interval 3–0 up with goals from Horton, Ward and 'Magic' Gerry Ryan. Inevitably they relaxed in the second half, but a late Newcastle consolation goal did nothing to dampen the celebrations on the south coast.

98

Cameroon 3   Nigeria 1
African Nations Cup final
Houphouet Boigny Abidjan, attendance 50,000
18 March 1984

Before wiggling his way to superstardom at Italia 90, this was Roger Milla's finest hour, inspiring Cameroon to African Nations victory against the brilliant up and coming Nigerians. Nigeria were young and inexperienced and, unlike their opponents, they had no seasoned professionals in their team. In the end that lack of experience told, but they started like cheetahs out of a drainpipe and took the lead after ten minutes.

It was a cracking match, both teams always looking to attack. Nigeria were young, quick and skilful but Cameroon, with the powerful Ndjeya (known as the 'Cameroon wardrobe' because of his height and strength) outstanding up front and driven on by Milla, even then a veteran (who for once he failed to score). Ndjeya brought the scores level in the thirty-second minute, but it wasn't until the seventy-ninth that Abega put Cameroon in the driving seat. With Nigeria streaming forward and the wily Cameroons trying to stifle the game, in the end it was the Indomitable Lions who scored again in the last minute. Six years later Roger Milla burst on to the world scene at Italia 90. You should have seen him when he was at his peak!

99

Manchester United 0   Southampton 1
FA Cup final
Wembley Stadium, attendance 100,000
5 May 1976

his is the sort of match the FA Cup was made for.
Lawrie McMenemy's Southampton, from the
Second Division, had had a glorious Cup run and
were rewarded with the most glamorous tie possible in
the final. Not many expected them to beat Manchester
United, even though most of the country hoped for it.

Tommy Docherty fielded a United team playing an
attack-minded 4–2–4 formation, but the only time they
really threatened to score was when an early Sammy
McIlroy header hit the woodwork. As the match progressed United faded as a force and Southampton, with
Jim McAlliog dominating in midfield, began to believe
their dream could become reality. Before the match
McMenemy had told his team, 'I don't care if the Queen
is watching, if it's dangerous, belt it into the Tyne.'
Instead they passed the ball round like the best of them.
On sixty-two minutes, the Doc replaced winger Gordon
Hill with the battling McCreery. But it was McAlliog,
sold from United the season before, who turned the
match, laying on a perfectly weighted pass to find Bobby
Stokes running free on goal. Stokes kept his head, hit a

low shot past the keeper, and scored with just seven minutes remaining. Little Bobby Stokes was an unlikely hero in a team which included Mick Channon and Peter Osgood, but a popular one. He won a car for his historic goal which brought Southampton their first trophy in ninety-one years. Pity he couldn't drive.

100

Antwerp 0   Newcastle 5
Uefa Cup first round, first leg
Bosuil Stadium, attendance 19,700
13 September 1993

Just over two years after avoiding relegation from the (old) Second Division by the skin of their teeth, Kevin Keegan's Newcastle United gave a very good impression of being one of the best teams in the continent on a barmy, balmy late summer night in Belgium.

In what was their first campaign in Europe for seventeen years, United simply thrashed an Antwerp side which had got to the final of the Cup Winners' Cup two years previously in a performance the Belgian manager Urbain Haersaert called 'the best display of quick-passing football I have ever seen'. And in-form Andy Cole didn't even manage to get on the score sheet! Robert Lee nodded a hat-trick of headers – an amazing feat for a midfield player – and Peter Beardsley and Steve Watson supplied the other goals. Incredibly, when they went into the half-time interval 3–0 up, Newcastle had not only the game but the whole tie sewn up and the 4,000 Geordies who'd crossed the Channel to see their heroes were justifiably over the Toon.

In the return leg Newcastle scored five again, but

conceded two, a portent for the defensive laxness that was to allow Atletico Bilbao to knock them out of the competition in the next round after they'd gone 3–0 down at St James's Park.

All Pan Books are available at your local bookshop or newsagent, or can be ordered direct from the publisher. Indicate the number of copies required and fill in the form below.

Send to: Macmillan General Books C.S.
               Book Service By Post
               PO Box 29, Douglas I-O-M
               IM99 1BQ

or phone: 01624 675137, quoting title, author and credit card number.

or fax: 01624 670923, quoting title, author, and credit card number.

or Internet: http://www.bookpost.co.uk

Please enclose a remittance* to the value of the cover price plus 75 pence per book for post and packing. Overseas customers please allow £1.00 per copy for post and packing.

*Payment may be made in sterling by UK personal cheque, Eurocheque, postal order, sterling draft or international money order, made payable to Book Service By Post.

Alternatively by Access/Visa/MasterCard

Card No.

Expiry Date

Signature

Applicable only in the UK and BFPO addresses.

While every effort is made to keep prices low, it is sometimes necessary to increase prices at short notice. Pan Books reserve the right to show on covers and charge new retail prices which may differ from those advertised in the text or elsewhere.

NAME AND ADDRESS IN BLOCK CAPITAL LETTERS PLEASE

Name

Address

8/95

Please allow 28 days for delivery.
Please tick box if you do not wish to receive any additional information. ☐